The INDIAN OCEAN and the THREAT to the WEST

FOUR STUDIES IN GLOBAL STRATEGY

Anthony Harrigan

Patrick Wall

The Institute for the Study of Conflict

W.A.C. Adie

edited by PATRICK WALL

STACEY INTERNATIONAL

ISBN 0 9503304 3 4 hardback

ISBN 0 9503304 4 2 paperback

First published by Stacey International 1975

©Stacey International and Anthony Harrigan, the Institute for the Study of Conflict, Patrick Wall and W A C Adie
All rights reserved. No part of this publication may be reproduced, stored in retrieval system, or transmitted in any form or by any means, electronic, mechanical, photocopying, recording or otherwise, without the prior permission of the copyright holders.

Stacey International, 128 Kensington Church Street, LONDON W8 4BH

distributed by
Bayard Books, Mercury House, Waterloo Road, LONDON SE1 8UL.

Printed and bound in Great Britain by
Redwood Burn Limited, Trowbridge & Esher

CONTENTS

List of Maps and Illustrations   7

    Foreword   9

    Patrick Wall

An American view
    Security Interests in the Persian Gulf and Western Indian Ocean   19

    Anthony Harrigan

A British and W European view
    The West and South Africa   39

    Patrick Wall

Middle Eastern factors
    The Security of the Cape Oil Route   67

    Institute for the Study of Conflict

An Australian view
    Strategic Problems in the Indian Ocean area   139

    W A C Adie

    Recent Developments and Conclusions   165

    Patrick Wall.

Appendices   183
Glossary   187
Index   189

Security Interests in the Persian Gulf was first published by the United States Strategic Institute; The Security of the Cape Oil Route by the Institute for the Study of Conflict; and Strategic Problems in the Indian Ocean by the Lugano Review.

Cover and design Richard Kelly

Cartography Christopher Fayers

Photographs Keystone Press, Associated Press

LIST OF MAPS

Rival naval and air facilities and or influences	16-17
Africa 1947 and 1975: the colonial withdrawal	42-43
Soviet and Chinese diplomatic representation in Africa	63
Soviet intelligence services representation in the Middle East and Africa	110-111

LIST OF ILLUSTRATIONS between pages 96-7

B J Vorster of South Africa
E G Whitlam of Australia
Julius Nyerere of Tanzania
Mrs Indira Gandhi of India
Ahmad Hassan al Bakr of Iraq
A Soviet naval squadron in the Indian Ocean 1974
A Soviet repair ship in the Indian Ocean 1974
A Soviet oceanographic research ship in the Indian Ocean 1974
A Soviet guided missile cruiser in the Indian Ocean 1974
Sheikh Mujibur Rahman of Bangladesh
Mrs S D Bandaranaike of Sri Lanka
Z A Bhutto of Pakistan
Sir Seewoosagur Ramgoolam of Mauritius
Lee Kuan Yew of Singapore
General Jaafar al Nimeiri of Sudan
Ahmed Zaki of Maldive Islands
General Siad Barre of Somalia
Jomo Kenyatta of Kenya
Joaqim Chissano of Mozambique
The Shah of Iran
Anwar al Sadat of Egypt
Salem Roubia Ali of South Yemen
King Faisal of Saudi Arabia
Sultan Qaboos of Oman

FOREWORD

THE HISTORY of Southern Africa is a story of sea power. The dominant maritime nations — first the Portugese, then the Dutch, the French and the British — discovered, traded with and colonised various parts of the African continent. From there Western ships sailed to their true goal, the Indian Ocean and the great riches in raw materials and minerals to be found along its shores.

For more than a century Britain's Navy probed those seas, putting an end to the slave trade and maintaining the *Pax Britannica*, within which the nations of the area developed their political and economic systems. Since the end of the Second World War, the U.S. Navy has largely taken over the role which the Royal Navy used to play, and many nations of Africa and Asia have become independent.

Now, it seems, the West has forgotten altogether about the importance of sea power, and is watching supinely while the world's greatest land power starts to dominate the sea as well. The Cuban crisis of 1962 taught the Russians a lesson; they are determined not to be caught in the same weak position again. The Soviet Navy, which was once hardly more than a coastal defence force, is rapidly becoming the most formidable fleet across the oceans of the world. The Kremlin fully understands the political advantages which sea power confers.

This new phenomenon, and especially its effect on the security of the West's oil supplies are examined in the following pages by three writers — Patrick Wall, Anthony Harrigan and Ian Adie. The particular importance of the Cape Route is discussed in a report from the Institute for the Study of Conflict, presided over by Brian Crozier.

Patrick Wall served in the Royal Navy, and for the past twenty years has been a Member of Britain's Parliament; he has made frequent visits to Africa and the Middle East; defence is his special interest. Anthony Harrigan is an

American journalist, a former editor of the *Charlestown Examiner;* he has written a number of books on political and military subjects, and knows Africa well. Ian Adie is a senior Research Fellow in International Relations at the Australian National University, Canberra; he has travelled widely in South-East Asia, India and China, and has written several books about Soviet and Chinese foreign policy. The Institute for the Study of Conflict was founded in 1970 and is based in London; it has issued a series of distinguished and influential reports.

These four papers were prepared separately and without any comparison of notes or sources. They are written from different points of view — British, American and Australian: but they come to the same conclusions and stress the same increasing dangers which the West will face during the next decade.

Despite the coming together of nine countries in the enlarged European Economic Community, Western Europe is still far from united, particularly over foreign policy. Her military experts see only too clearly the risk which flows from dependence on Middle East oil and the long haul round the Cape: but the politicians, obsessed by the unpopularity with "world opinion" of South Africa, Rhodesia and, until recently, Portugal, refuse to grasp the strategic facts. In the last resort, they believe, the South Africans would be bound to side with the West. But by then it may be too late.

Leftward-leaning Western Governments enthusiastically abuse, and try to boycott, South Africa and Rhodesia. At the same time, without seeing any inconsistency, they advocate an expansion of trade and closer cultural links with the Soviet Union and her satellites. The next ten years may well be the period of greatest danger: a period during which the West will continue to be dependent on oil from the Middle East, while Soviet sea-power, compared to that of NATO, will achieve its maximum advantage. After this period, other sources of energy and new oil supplies should make the West less vulnerable.

The American point of view is rather different. The United States is much less dependent on Middle East oil, and is still, to some extent, regarded as the world's policeman. Americans have every right to complain about Europe's failure to assume a fair share of the defence burden. The decision by Britain's Labour Government to withdraw altogether from the Gulf certainly increased the peril. If Britain now decides to pull out of the Indian Ocean entirely, the American Government will come under increasing pressure from its own electors, who want to see the military budget pruned. But, as Mr Harrigan points out, although oil from the Gulf supplied, until recently, only three per cent of America's needs, this figure has already increased sharply and may have risen to thirty-five per cent by 1979; hence America's new concern about the Indian Ocean, where the Soviet Union already holds so many key points within its sphere of influence.

The Australians have an even more direct interest in the eastern reaches of the Indian Ocean. They identify themselves increasingly with the South East Asian area; a process accelerated by their present Labour Government — which is deliberately loosening the old links with Britain and the United States, while cultivating closer relations with Communist China and Indonesia.

As all the writers in this book emphasise, the strategic advantages enjoyed by the Western Allies during the Second World War have virtually disappeared. The Soviet Union, on the other hand, now enjoys naval facilities in Ceylon (Sri Lanka) and India, Aden, Socotra, the Somali Republic, at Umm Qasr in Iraq and possibly in the Andaman and Nicobar Islands, and at various other anchorages throughout the area. At the moment, however, the Russians still lack military airfields, although they have had bombers, long-range reconnaissance planes and fighters based on Egyptian airfields, and might have the use of Syrian and Iraqi airfields, or those in Aden or the Somali Republic.

Air cover in the Southern Indian Ocean and the South Atlantic would be difficult for them to provide; their planes would have to operate from Aden and from Conakry in Guinea.

The West is comparatively better placed. Apart from the

facilities in Southern Africa, the RAF has military airfields at Masira and Gan; there are good commercial airfields in Mauritius and the Seychelles; and Diego Garcia may soon be developed.

No naval dockyards are available to the West between Simonstown and Singapore: and the future even of Singapore will become doubtful if the five-power Commonwealth force is withdrawn. The French still have facilities at Diego Suarez, but these may not last much longer. The US Navy has minor facilities in Bahrain, but has been given notice to quit. The continued availability of friendly ports and airfields in Southern Africa is, therefore, vital.

The report by the Institute for the Study of Conflict examines in detail the strategic situation in the key area of the Gulf, emphasising the importance of Saudi Arabia, both as a leading Arab power and as an oil producer. Equally important is the stabilising effect of Iran, which is rapidly becoming one of the best equipped military powers in the Middle East. The risk of guerilla warfare sparked by such organisations as the Palestine Liberation Organisation, the Popular Front for the Liberation of Oman and the Arabian Gulf (PFLOAG), which is based in Aden, or of sabotage attacks on tankers in the Gulf ports, may not be very great, but the growth of Soviet influence, both directly through Governments and indirectly through workers' organisations, should certainly not be underestimated.

There appears to be little immediate danger of an open Soviet move into the Gulf, but the possibility of a threat, whether direct or indirect, to the West's oil supply routes is real. It could be exerted through some third country, in order to make Russia's part less obvious.

In the light of these perils, the security of Southern Africa becomes even more important to the West; but that security is already under attack by guerilla movements, which enjoy considerable support from other nations — including some in Western Europe. The effect of these guerilla movements is examined in this book, the conclusion being that, in the short term, they are unlikely to disrupt the stability of South

Africa, provided external factors such as Dr. Banda's policy of non-intervention does not change and the political will of the Lisbon government to continue Portugal's role in Africa remains firm. The situation is completely altered by the rapid volte-face in Portugal and the decision of the new government to hand over Mozambique to FRELIMO. The transition may however not prove to be peaceful due to the rivalry between the Macua and Maconde tribes.

A very interesting passage in the report by The Institute for the Study of Conflict explains the objectives of Soviet and Chinese policies. Tactics and methods have changed, but the objectives have not. These continue to be, in the long term, the fostering of Marxist regimes subservient to Moscow or Peking, and, in the medium term, the establishment of client states, dependent upon Soviet or Chinese arms and advisers.

The reader must judge for himself how far these aims have already been achieved: but clearly the two great Communist Powers have stepped into the vacuum created by Britain's withdrawal. Client states — Iraq, Syria, Egypt, the Somali Republic, South Yemen, Guinea — have been created. American influence in the Middle East has been drastically reduced. The Suez Canal is soon to be re-opened, which will be of great advantage to the Soviet Fleet. Russia's capacity to affect the vital supply of oil to the West has increased.

Few, if any, African states can really be called pro-Western. The majority are unaligned but responsive to Soviet or Chinese penetration. Mozambique has now been surrendered to the anti-Western camp. Angola may follow. The future of the Cape Verde Islands is not yet clear. The prospect before the Western World would be very dangerous indeed if "non-aligned" Governments, friendly to the Soviet Union or to China, were to be set up in South Africa and Rhodesia. Yet this is exactly what so many Western politicians and political or humanitarian groups seem to want and to be actively encouraging.

Britain had no better friend than Sir Abubakar Belewa, a great African statesman and the first leader of independent

Nigeria. Yet before the first year of independence was over, he had been forced to repudiate the Anglo-Nigerian defence treaty. A few years later he was murdered. This demonstrates the pressures that exist in so many newly independent nations to remain unaligned.

Let us bear in mind, too, the quotation from *Pravda* (22nd August 1973) mentioned in the report of The Institute for the Study of Conflict: "Peaceful co-existence does not spell an end to the struggle between the two world social systems. The struggle will continue between the proletariat and the bourgeoisie, between world socialism and imperialism, up to the complete and final victory of communism on a world scale."

Lenin believed that the Western democracies would destroy themselves from within through becoming soft, greedy and lacking in will power. He may yet prove to have been right.

Patrick Wall

Rival Naval and Air Facilities

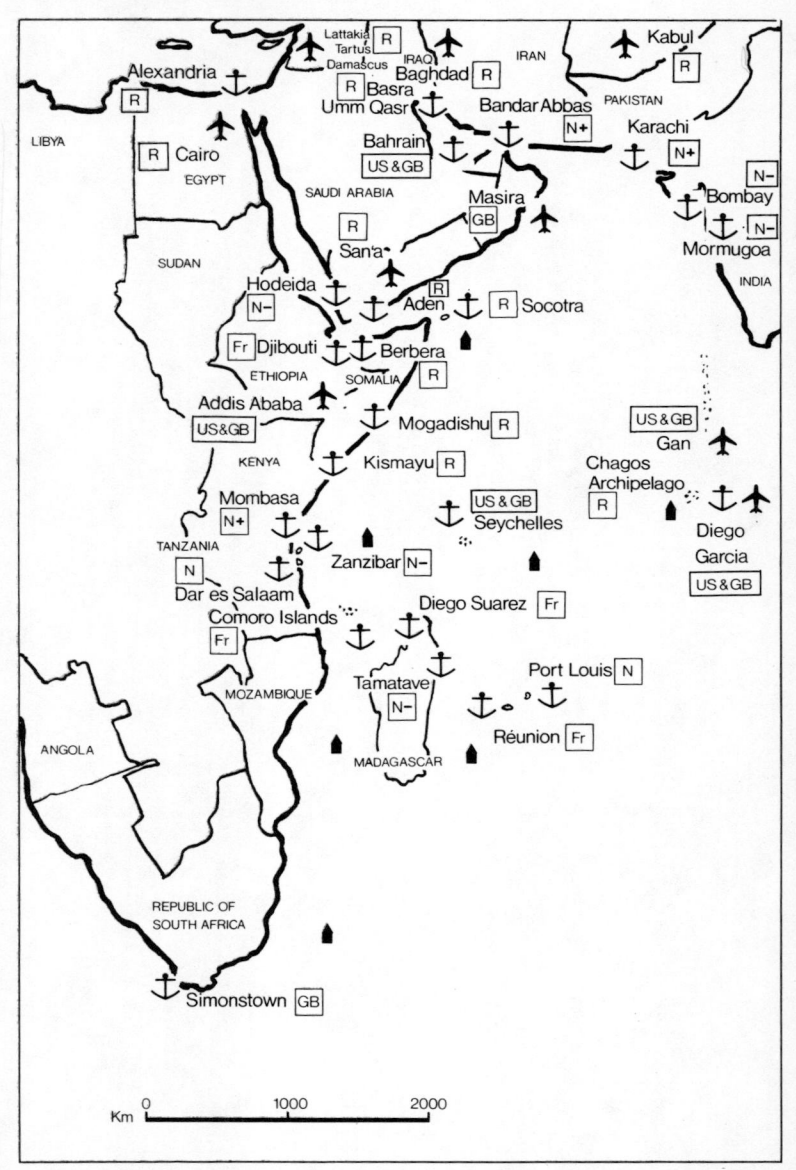

An azimuthal projection. All mooring buoys have been placed and are used by Soviet vessels only.

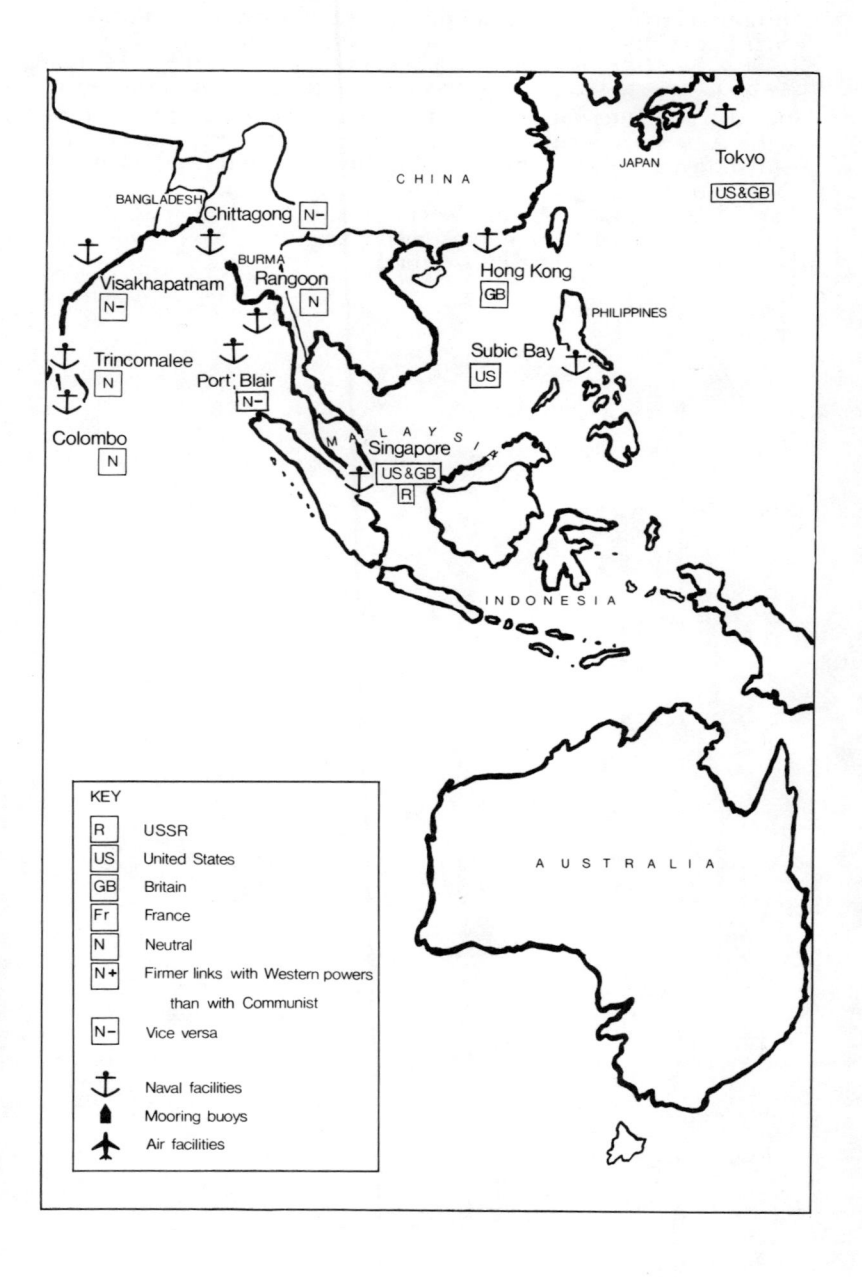

FOREWORD

Anthony Harrigan is a former newspaper editor and the author of seven books on military and national affairs, including *Defence Against Total Attack* and *A Guide to the War in Vietnam*. He is a former Research Associate at the Georgetown University Centre of Strategic and International Studies and former Managing Editor of the American Security Council's *Washington Report*. He has contributed widely to professional military journals in the United States and in allied countries. He has lectured at the U.S. National War College, South African Defence College and other academic institutions. Since 1970, he has been Executive Vice President of the United States Industrial Council.

Anthony Harrigan

SECURITY INTERESTS IN THE PERSIAN GULF AND WESTERN INDIAN OCEAN

SINCE THE opening of the twentieth century, the Atlantic and Pacific Oceans have been the primary theatres of history for the people of the United States. Two world wars and lesser conflicts have been fought on those oceans and on the continents they separate. As we approach the final quarter of the twentieth century, however, it is increasingly clear that the Indian Ocean is becoming the new arena of political conflict. More particularly, one of the arms of that ocean — the 500-mile long Persian Gulf — has become a focus of our strategic concerns.

The vastness of this ocean region is little comprehended by the U.S. public. The entire Indian Ocean is 4,000 miles wide by 4,000 miles long. One statistic indicates the scope of the naval security problems involved in this region. From Durban, South Africa to Aden, at the entrance to the Red Sea, is a distance of 3,275 miles. The sea frontier from Aden on the Arabian Peninsula to the Gulf of Oman is more than 1,200 miles. The Western Indian Ocean, the area of special concern to the United States and the NATO countries, embraces the Arabian Sea — the waters between Arabia and India — and a vast stretch of ocean to the south in which are located several major island groups. It has been an ocean of destiny since the dawn of history, with Indians, Chinese, Romans, Arabs and many other peoples trading and waging war on its reaches.

The source of the conflict today can be encapsuled in a single word: oil. The energy needs of the industrialized Northern Hemisphere countries dictate a profound concern with access to the oil resources of the Persian Gulf (more than sixty per cent of the world's proven reserves) and with the security of the tanker routes through the Gulf and across the Western Indian Ocean in time of war or political crisis.

Widespread concern with the Persian Gulf and Western Indian Ocean dates from comparatively recent times in the United States and in the NATO countries. In 1967, when Great Britain began to withdraw from its bastions east of Suez, the Persian Gulf was virtually a British lake. Britain maintained key control points in the Indian Ocean from Aden in the west to Singapore in the east. But within a year of the British withdrawal, which created a power vacuum, the Soviet Union began to dispatch strong naval forces into the Indian Ocean. Iraq, at the head of the Persian Gulf, is now a Soviet client state. The Soviets have facilities at Indian ports. As the result of various agreements, they have access to ports in Aden, Somalia and Mauritius. Indeed almost all the control points in the Western Indian Ocean — Zanzibar on the East African coast, Socotra at the entrance to the Red Sea, Madagascar, Ceylon (Sri Lanka) — are in the hands of powers hostile to the West. Of these extensive British strong points, only the Cape of Good Hope — the "Bastion of the South" — remains under anti-Communist Western control.

It was from these shore and island positions that Great Britain dominated the Indian Ocean world. The Soviet Union is well on its way to controlling or influencing the nations that hold the majority of these key points. The only recent gain by the West — and it is a very modest gain — is the development of a U..S. Navy communications station on the British island of Diego Garcia south of the Indian subcontinent. This small station helps close a gap in America's worldwide communications system. But in no sense is it a major naval base. The 8,000 foot runway on Diego Garcia is an element — but only a single element — in the network of airfields the West needs in order to deploy aerial might in the region in the event of a crisis. Satellites provide intelligence data, but any lengthy interruption of surface shipping or other hostile action would require deployment of tactical aircraft appropriate to the situation.

Our Dependence on Oil

It is the danger of interrupted oil movements that gives concern in the United States, Europe and Japan. The most vulnerable country is Japan. Almost ninety per cent of its energy comes from the Persian Gulf. An oil embargo or interruption of tanker traffic would shut down Japanese industrial production and plunge the world's third strongest economy into crisis. While the Japanese seek new oil sources in Indonesia and Australia and are pushing ahead with nuclear power plant construction, their dependence on the Persian Gulf will continue well into the 1980s.

Europe's dependence is almost as great. Japan and Europe together import more than 700 million gallons of oil per day from the Persian Gulf. European imports from the Gulf are expected to increase 450 per cent over the next decade, despite development of the North Sea oil and gas fields and French advances in nuclear technology. The figures are revealing.[1] Britain obtains 66.1 per cent of her oil from the Gulf states, Italy 84.5 per cent, France 51.1 per cent and West Germany 62 per cent. Australia, which gets 69 per cent of its oil from the Persian Gulf, also has a tremendous security stake in the area.

Until recently, the Persian Gulf was not a significant source of energy for the United States, with only three per cent coming from that source. Over the next five years, however, imports from the Gulf may account for twenty-five per cent of U.S. oil supplies despite the U.S. goal of energy sufficiency.[2] The dollar drain for these Persian Gulf oil purchases already is enormous. A total of $2.1 billion was spent for Middle East oil in 1970. The Petroleum Council estimates of costs range from $9 billion to $13 billion in 1985. This is not surprising, however, in view of the fact that the United States is the largest consumer of petroleum in the world.

Given the projected size and cost of the Persian Gulf oil imports, it is no wonder that the Gulf and the Western

Indian Ocean suddenly have become very significant areas to the United States. Drew Middleton, Military Editor of the *New York Times*, has said that[3] "Military planners expect that the strategic interests of the United States and global strategy in general will pivot on the Persian Gulf late in this decade as a result of competition for the area's oil."

It already has been a shock to many Americans to realize the extent of their growing dependency on energy from this remote, unstable, and often hostile part of the world. Before long, the American government and people are likely to find this dependency intolerable. The United States, as a result, should move ahead on a crash basis to develop its domestic energy sources — to expand coal production, to institute new coal gasification methods, to open Arctic and offshore oil fields, to extract oil from shale and sands, which exist in vast quantities in North America, and to accelerate progress toward fast breeder nuclear reactors and the fusion process. Faced by great challenges, the United States has shown the capacity to work scientific, engineering and economic miracles. In all likelihood, however, it will take the United States a decade to augment its domestic energy sources to the point where it need not be vastly concerned about oil imports. In the meantime, the United States will be dependent on oil from the Persian Gulf that is moved by tanker across the Western Indian Ocean.

In this connection, it is pertinent to note the danger of proposals that the United States should by its own investment policy become dependent upon imports of Soviet fuels, as the Federal Republic of Germany is doing. Such action would give hostage to an enemy for our future behaviour.

William F. Case, an oil expert with the U.S. Department of Transportation, has drawn the conclusion that "if events are allowed to follow a natural course, the United States will almost certainly face an eight to ten year period beginning in 1975-77 of critical dependence on Middle East oil."

For Western Europe, the dependence may last considerably longer — until the atomic fusion process is perfected and working on a large scale. Few Western states are free of major worries with respect to energy. Ironically, one of these is an Indian Ocean country without any oil. As the *South African Financial Gazette* has pointed out:[4]

> South Africa, with its vast, readily available coal reserves, is in the vanguard of countries determined to be self-sufficient in its energy resources, and can regard the present situation with a degree of equanimity... In the case of South Africa, its oil from coal production know-how and huge coal and uranium reserves render it much less vulnerable than most Western nations to the inevitable fuel price increases of the near future.

Shaping a Strategy

The United States and the NATO countries are not in this happy situation, however, and must develop an overall strategy for maintaining access to Persian Gulf oil. And although the United States played the major role in developing oil in Saudi Arabia, it is at a severe disadvantage in shaping a politico-military strategy for the period ahead, in which it must have access to oil from the Gulf.

First, there is the problem of distance. The only U.S. facilities in the area are the communications stations at Diego Garcia and at Northwest Cape in Australia. Indeed the U.S. position in Australia may be insecure in view of the increasingly pacifist policy of the current Australian government.

America's overseas base structure was designed for conflicts in the Atlantic and Pacific, not for the remote Indian Ocean. The well-equipped naval base at Simonstown at the Cape of Good Hope is a useful facility for American warships, but the Johnson Administration ordered a halt to U.S. ship visits to South African ports and ended the joint naval exercises that had been standard procedure during the Eisenhower Administration. This policy of snubbing a vital, technologically advanced ally in the Indian Ocean remains in force.

It is doubtful that the United States could maintain adequate naval and air contingents in the Western Indian

Ocean without recourse to Simonstown. Deployment of ships and aircraft from the United States to the Indian Ocean requires a huge investment in dollars and manpower. Dr. Alvin J. Cottrell, Director of Research for the Centre for Strategic and International Studies at Georgetown University, has noted:[5]

> Some people talk about a modest increase of two U.S. ships at Bahrein (in the Persian Gulf), which would be possible under the established ceiling. But to put two more ships there, we would need a total of twelve ships. Sending them all the way from the East Coast of the United States means a requirement of 3:1 in terms of ships on station to ships en route and being readied.

Some observers may question whether a limited U.S. commitment of ships would so alter the power balance in the Western Indian Ocean as to add significantly to U.S. security in the area or to enhance the protection of the oil traffic in which the United States is vitally interested. Time and again throughout the post-World War period the Soviets have been checked in their ambitions by a limited U.S. presence. Certainly, the U.S. Berlin garrison could not stop a serious Soviet assault. The embarked battalion of U.S. Marines in the Mediterranean is a token force compared to what the Soviets could quickly muster in the area. In practice, the Soviets have been unwilling to risk a major confrontation involving U.S. armed forces, whatever their size, whereas they might be tempted to risk a *fait accompli* in the Western Indian Ocean in the absence of any U.S. naval forces. Moreover, the deployment of a limited U.S. force would be essential in inducing other Western nations to make commitments of forces to a greater allied presence.

Recognizing that the great powers will be drawn more and more into the Indian Ocean, it is necessary to consider also the respective possibilities for the deployment of Free World and Communist airpower. As mentioned earlier, the U.S. facility on Diego Garcia in the middle of the Indian Ocean provides only a very limited capability for handling aircraft, though a small number of reconnaissance flights could be made from the island. What would be needed in a crisis situation, however, would be airfields closer to the major sea lanes. The airfields in Western Australia, though available, are far removed from the danger points. The airfield of Perth, for example, is approximately 5,000 miles from Aden.

Fortunately, the Iranians have pushed airfield construction. At present, they have military jet fields at Bushire, Kish and Bandar Abbas on the Persian Gulf of Oman near the Pakistan border. This base will be ideally situated to provide air cover for ships operating in the Arabian Sea.

The French have important airfields at Djibouti on the Gulf of Aden and on Reunion Island 400 miles east of Madagascar. Djibouti is especially important because (given French cooperation with the United States and other Western countries) aircraft based there could monitor ocean areas around the Horn of Africa and south along the coast of Somalia. Diego Suarez, the former French naval base on Madagascar, would be of tremendous value to the West in any naval confrontation or oil movement crisis in the Indian Ocean. At this time, however, access to naval bases and airfields in the Malagasy Republic is not available. Obtaining access to these facilities should be a priority political objective for the oil-consuming nations of the West.

The decision of the Portuguese to withdraw from Mozambique is a very serious setback to Western interests. Up to early 1974 there was some reason to hope that ports and airfields in Mozambique might become available to the West in time of crisis in the Indian Ocean. But the radically altered political situation in that territory eliminates that possibility.

Given the revolutionary change in Mozambique, the United States will have to take a new look at the possibility of defence coordination with the Republic of South Africa.

Indeed, co-ordination with Portugal's successors and the Republic of South Africa is imperative if the tanker traffic is to be safeguarded on both the Indian Ocean approaches to the Cape of Good Hope and in the adjacent South Atlantic area. South Africa has a significant navy, equipped with modern French submarines, British-built frigates and a variety of other ships and weapons. It possesses a truly modern communications headquarters at Simonstown, capable of monitoring ship movements through a large area of the Western Indian Ocean. It has a network of fully modern airbases, plus supporting aircraft facilities, throughout its coastal zones. Its air force is equipped with French Mirage fighters and other superlative equipment, lacking only long-range maritime aircraft. All elements of the South African defence forces are in a high state of combat readiness. They could play a key role in any situation involving a threat to oil lifelines of the Western countries.

In the event of a major crisis, it must be assumed that the Soviet Union could execute a forward deployment of its own involving dispatch of aircraft to Aden, India and Somalia. Tanzania is oriented towards Peking rather than Moscow, and the Chinese Communists have been building a military airfield near Dar-es-Salaam; but Soviet access to that airfield cannot be ruled out in view of Tanzania's stance against the Western powers.

The deployment of U.S. naval vessels and/or squadrons is not a substitute for a national strategy covering the Western Indian Ocean. The situation has changed completely since the days when the British were dominant in the area. Aside from the Soviet naval presence, which consists of a substantial task force of approximately a dozen or more modern ships, there are the rapidly expanding military capabilities of several littoral nations plus the problem of serious subversion and insurgency in others. Thus, the Western Indian Ocean area equation gets more complicated year by year.

Conflict Situations

In the Gulf itself — the immediate, vital zone — there are numerous tensions and deeply rooted problems: disputes over undersea boundaries, the Iranian claim to Bahrain, Iraq's threatening actions toward Kuwait, a subversive mini-war in Dhofar, Saudi hankerings after parts of Abu Dhabi and Oman. Each of these disputes could have a trigger effect on a conflict involving external powers.

The major conflict situation, however, involves Iraq and Iran. On April 9, 1972, Iraq entered into a treaty of friendship with the Soviet Union, which provides for military cooperation. Iran, on the other hand, is linked to the United States and is currently in the midst of a significant military build-up. The Iranian armed forces are being equipped with the latest United States and British weapons, including F-4 Phantom jets and Hovercraft assault vehicles. The Shah has evidenced strong determination to make Iran the leading Persian Gulf power and to control ship traffic through the Straits of Hormuz. In addition, he envisages Iran's security perimeter extending beyond the straits into the Indian Ocean.

A complication has been added in the form of an Indian training mission to Iraq that trains Iraqi pilots to fly Soviet-supplied MIG fighters. The participation of the Indians in the training scheme is another indication of India's close collaboration with the Soviet Union in trying to eliminate all Western influence from the Indian Ocean.

The Indian government denies that it has given facilities to the Soviet Navy on India's coasts or outlying islands. But the denial fails to convince many observers who note the presence of numerous Soviet naval advisers and the transfer of Soviet ships to India. Hanson W. Baldwin wrote in his book, *Strategy for Tomorrow*, regarding the common features of Soviet and Indian military and naval planning. He noted[6] that the first steps had been taken for the "integration" of the Indian military establishment with the Soviet.

In another decade, given conditions of peace, Iran will have attained a very considerable degree of industrialization. Reforms introduced by the Shah are designed to bring Iran fully into the modern world. But the next decade will be fraught with difficulties and dangers because of the weakness and vulnerability of the small states on the Arabian peninsula and because of Communist-inspired insurgency. The Union of Arab Emirates, composed of seven small states, is very weak. It is subject to subversive pressure from both Soviet and Chinese Communist elements in the so-called Popular Front for the Liberation of Oman and the Arab Gulf. This type of subversive activity can be found almost anywhere along the rim of the western Indian Ocean — from the Eritrean Liberation Front in Ethiopia to the FRELIMO terrorist organization in Mozambique, an organization dominated by pro-Peking elements, which today appears to have inherited the Portuguese mantle.

Current American concern with respect to the western Indian Ocean is almost completely related to the need for adequate oil supplies. But no appraisal of the area would be complete without mention of the Chinese Communist penetration of Tanzania on the East African coast and the operation of terrorists against Mozambique and Rhodesia. These terrorist groups, with their parallel sanctuaries in Tanzania and Zambia, look to the Chinese Communist construction of the Tan-Zam Railroad as an instrument for creating a Red belt across Central Africa from Tanzania on the Indian Ocean to Zaire's window on the South Atlantic.

While the primary U.S. emphasis on the Indian Ocean has to do with oil, strategic planners cannot ignore the fact that the United States depends on Indian Ocean routes for access to strategic minerals and materials in Africa, including beryl, chrome, ore, antimony, asbestos, copper, columbium, lead, nickel and uranium. The United States is not only facing an energy crisis in the mid and late 1970s but a minerals crisis as well. Access to strategic minerals will be an increasingly serious national concern in the latter part of this decade. The same situation applies to the NATO countries, of course. Africa has been a source of essential minerals for Europe. The security of the Indian Ocean route is of prime importance to Europe, especially with respect to the movement of copper.

On top of all the national rivalries and confusion of states and political movements on the rim of the western Indian Ocean there is the problem of the Arab-Israeli contest. Emotional and religious issues have become involved in the struggle over oil, for example, as the Arab nations debate the curtailment of oil supply as a means of altering American and West European policies on the Arab-Israeli confrontation. No more complicated problem has confronted U.S. statesmen and military planners than that of devising an overall policy designed to protect America's vital interests in the western Indian Ocean world.

The Psychological Factor

A further complication — and it is one that the U.S. public must recognize — is that the threatened loss of energy sources in a remote region comes at a time when a mood of withdrawal is dominant in the United States and when Congress and many citizens oppose foreign involvements of any sort. Add to this the intensity of the anti-defence campaign conducted by some elements of the media and one gets an outline of the restrictions inhibiting U.S. policy planners in devising an appropriate response to the dangers emerging in the western Indian Ocean.

The threat, of course, is real and clear — politically ordained cut-offs of oil that the U.S. Europe and Japan must have and/or a combination of insurgency and Soviet naval support for revolutionary elements bent on overthrowing Persian Gulf governments that are reasonably friendly to the United States. Faced with threats in the Atlantic and Pacific in recent years (Dominican Republic, Taiwan, etc.), the United States has had ready forces to intervene or to bar enemy intervention. But the U.S. is without effective forces in the western Indian Ocean. It has only a token, show-the-flag contingent of two ships in the Persian Gulf.

This would not be the first time that the mood of the American public and Congress has deterred the U.S. from taking measures necessary to provide for national security. The isolationism that followed World War I effectively prevented the United States from opposing Japan's militarization of the former German islands in the Pacific north of the equator. This American passivity resulted in a shift in the strategic balance and encouraged Imperial Japan to strike at the United States in 1941.

This experience is applicable to developing conditions in the Persian Gulf and western Indian Ocean. The U.S. has a tremendous strategic interest in the oil-production and resulting maritime commerce, but it may lack the means and the public will to interpose strong forces that would fully stabilize the area.

Some Security Imperative

Some additions to U.S. strength in the western Indian Ocean are imperative, however, if America is to maintain any degree of credibility as a power that can translate its words into deeds. Logically, the naval units assigned to the western Indian Ocean would be homeported at Simonstown. But considerations of politics in the United States would seem to rule out the adoption of this logical, pragmatic solution. The U.S. government would not be likely to order such homeporting in view of the certainty of an outcry from elements willing to sacrifice the nation's strategic interests for considerations of domestic politics and ideology.

Nevertheless, there is a possibility that a new formula could be devised that would permit a valuable coordination of air and naval operations involving surveillance of tanker traffic and Soviet warships. Practical ways might be found to combine U.S. and South African naval strengths in keeping the sea lanes open. American military aircraft do visit South African airfields from time to time. Joint naval manoeuvres were held to devise arrangements that would give U.S. forces the benefit of communications and technical facilities at Simonstown while affording South Africa new opportunities for coordination and receipt of maritime Intelligence data.

The augmentation of forces in the Indian Ocean would necessarily be modest, however, in view of the costs and the lack of a public policy. In the main, therefore, the U.S. in order to protect its interests, will have to rely on assistance to and cooperation with friendly powers in the area. It also will be vital for the U.S. to enter into cooperative arrangements with the principal West European powers which share our strategic stake in unrestricted access to and movement of the Persian Gulf oil.

The most important U.S. relationship in the area is with Iran, which is the premier power of the Gulf region and which has long-standing ties with the United States. As the Iranians make ever-greater use of American defence equipment and long-term commitments for training, spare parts and replacements, the bonds of alliance will be strengthened. These arrangements are eased in that Iran is not involved in a military confrontation with Israel. The historic Iranian strategic concern is with Soviet pressure from the north, now gaining a new dimension because of Soviet seapower in the Indian Ocean.

The other major Gulf power with which the United States needs to develop improved relations is Saudi Arabia. This task poses a greater problem for the United States because of the vulnerability of Saudi Arabia to pressure from more militant Arab countries. Saudi Arabia's great wealth makes it an object of envy in the Arab world. It is virtually forced to give financial aid to other Arab states as a device to buy peace. It must be borne in mind, moreover, that the revolutionary Arab states are ideologically opposed to the traditional system of government in Saudi Arabia. The vastness and relative emptiness of this desert country are an invitation to attack. Saudi Arabia has a population of about seven million scattered over a huge territory — 833,000 square miles, or a region about three times the size of Texas. Thus, Saudi Arabia has legitimate cause for anxiety about its security.

In these circumstances, the United States has done well to agree to sell arms to Saudi Arabia and adjacent Kuwait. The latter state, very small and enormously rich in oil revenues, is a prime target for revolutionary forces in the Arab world.

In selling arms to certain Arab nations *and* Israel, the United States government has emphasized what it calls a policy of evenhandedness. The goal — and it is a sound one — is a policy towards Saudi Arabia and Israel that combines friendliness with restraint. Pragmatic policy planners in the

United States know that even if a sharp tilt toward the Arab countries were desirable right now, the realities of domestic politics, as seen and accepted by successive administrations, render such a drastic change of course exceedingly unlikely. Thus, the U.S. approach must be one of modest adjustments, coupled with provision to Saudi Arabia of modern defence systems capable of coping with the offensive weapons that the Soviet Union furnishes to the revolutionary Arab nations. Anything less than this almost certainly would result in a future takeover of Saudi Arabia by revolutionary, anti-Western elements.

The European Interest

In devising plans to protect its interests in the Persian Gulf and western Indian Ocean, the United States also has to calculate the future role of the NATO countries. Three of these countries — Britain, France and Portugal — have a history of activity in the Indian Ocean. All retain interests in this oceanic theatre. France, for example, controls the small, highly strategic Afars and Issas territory at the mouth of the Red Sea and Reunion Island in the Indian Ocean. Britain continues to maintain limited naval forces between Cape Town and Singapore. Ships of the Royal Navy make regular calls at Simonstown naval base under terms of the 1955 Simonstown Agreement which provides joint naval security measures with South Africa. Together, the members of the North Atlantic Treaty Organization account for fifty-six per cent of the shipping (25,000 ships a year) that go around the Cape of Good Hope.

In summary, the NATO countries are dependent on the Cape Route and tanker traffic to the Persian Gulf. Yet there are no substantial or coordinated efforts by the West European nations to protect their interests in this crucial region. Patrick Wall, M.P., writing in NATO's *Fifteen Nations (The Hague),* has commented:

> This is of course absurd, but because of Western politicians' fears of becoming embroiled in the politics of

Southern Africa, NATO is not allowed to plan for the South Atlantic or South Indian Ocean.... What is sorely needed is official NATO recognition of the Simonstown Agreement and the provision of adequate communications and joint planning facilites.... Surely it is near lunacy not to make adequate provisions now.

Major Wall wrote those words a year or so prior to the West's sudden burst of concern about access to Persian Gulf oil. Today, the urgency of West European commitment to defence planning in the Western Indian Ocean is vastly greater. It is unlikely, however, that the needs of the situation will be met by NATO's ponderous consultative machinery. The commitment of ships to the Indian Ocean — and that's what is needed — most probably will have to be sought on a nation-by-nation basis. The West European nations which want to be sure they have access to Persian Gulf oil in the mid-seventies must be made to understand that the United States will not furnish security for their sea communications between the Cape of Good Hope and the Gulf.

No doubt it will be a shock to many West European nations to realize that they have a strategic requirement for deploying forces "East of Suez." These nations have come to depend on the United States to assume all the defence burdens in remote regions. But the financial cost of involvement in the Indian Ocean is nothing as compared to the shock that West European nations would experience if they found their customary oil supplies from the Gulf suddenly interrupted or terminated. In pressing for naval commitments from the West European nations, the United States will have to utilize stern diplomacy, linking the naval commitments in the new danger region to American force levels in Europe. In turn, the European nations undoubtedly would find that deployment of fleet units to the tanker routes and to the waters of the oil-producing countries would give their diplomatic efforts a new credibility.

This independent deployment of warships and supporting sea-based aircraft by several European nations may seem to be a rejection of alliance after two decades of the NATO experience. It is important, therefore, to remember that the warships of several West European countries operate in North European and Mediterranean waters without NATO control. France has been going her own way for some years. And in the Baltic, Danish, German and Swedish units operate independently, although all are concerned about the Soviet naval threat in those waters. In the Indian Ocean, U.S., British, French, Australian, South African and other Western countries maintain naval units wholly independent of one another. Independent operation can continue in the future. The real need is for immediate augmentation of Western naval forces and for coordination in time of crisis.

These proposed political and military measures constitute a feasible, albeit limited, initiative on the part of the United States and other Western nations. Compared to some of the actions the United States has taken in the past in Europe and South East Asia, the steps outlined here may seem overly cautious and restricted in scope. It would be desirable to develop at least one base under American control, and to deploy U.S. Air Force units in the area, but major undertakings of this sort don't appear feasible in the immediate, post-Vietnam era. Any suggestion of large-scale action wouldn't be a practical contribution to solving a serious, developing security problem. At this point in American history, only minimum commitments have a chance of winning congressional and public approval. Even the proposals for a limited commitment will probably be strenuously opposed. One can only hope that as the nation gains a clearer understanding of the dimensions of the threat to its energy sources, responsible leaders will be enabled to take prudent security measures.

"Wait-and-See" Won't Do

The shift of the global danger point from the great ocean basins of the Atlantic and Pacific was foreseen over a decade ago by two prescient American admirals, Arleigh Burke, former Chief of Naval Operations, and John S. McCain, Jr., former Commander-in-Chief Pacific. They warned numerous times of the need to establish a U.S. naval presence in the Indian Ocean.

The requirements of the Vietnam War put creation of an Indian Ocean task force temporarily beyond U.S. capabilities. Even as the war wound down, however, and the West began to get an inkling of the emerging energy crisis, American policy planners accorded the Indian Ocean a low priority. As late as 1971, Ronald Spiers, Director of the Bureau of Politico-Military Affairs of the Department of State, told the House Foreign Affairs Committee that "there appear to be no requirements at this time for us to feel compelled to control or even decisively influence any part of the Indian Ocean or its littoral." This statement was made at a time when the Soviet Union was sharply stepping up its deployment of naval forces in the Indian Ocean.

The "wait-and-see" policy of the U.S. with respect to the Indian Ocean has been overtaken by events. Political change in Madagascar has resulted in the removal of French influence. Tanzania has permitted the Chinese Communists to build a naval base that could be used by small missile-firing craft capable of interdicting tanker traffic. Elsewhere the situation has deteriorated drastically.

For the moment, the Persian Gulf nations possess an Aladdin's lamp of riches and international political leverage. By the end of this century, after the advanced Western nations have developed new energy processes on their territories, the oil-producing countries will cease to have a central position in world affairs. But, for the time being, the West cannot ignore the powerful genie in the oil wells of the Middle East. The United States and its allies in Western Europe must make certain that their political and military policies assure them access to the vital energy resources represented by Persian Gulf oil.

NOTES

1. Capt.A.P.S. Bindra, "The Indian Ocean As Seen by an Indian," *Proceedings of the U.S. Naval Institute*, May, 1970.
2. "U.S. Energy Outlook," National Petroleum Council, December, 1972.
3. The *New York Times*, April 20, 1973.
4. The *South African Financial Gazette*, May 11, 1973.
5. Dr. Alvin J.Cottrell, "The Soviet Presence and the Littoral States," *Conference Report on Economic and Political Development in Relation to Sea Power Along the Routes from the Indian Ocean*, National Strategy Information Center, New York, 1973, p.74.
6. Hanson Baldwin, *Strategy for Tomorrow*, Harper & Row, New York, 1970, p.212.

Patrick Wall is currently a vice-chairman of the Conservative Parliamentary Defence Committee, a member of the Military Committee of the North Atlantic Assembly, and a member of the Western European Union Defence Committee. As a British Member of Parliament he has specialised in defence and foreign affairs, and was vice-chairman of the Conservative Commonwealth Affairs Committee from 1960 to 1968, and of the Oversea Bureau from 1963 to 1973. He was a regular officer in the Royal Marines from 1935 to 1950, serving with the Royal Navy, the U.S. Navy and Commandos. He was awarded the Military Cross and the U.S. Legion of Merit. After the war he qualified at the Naval Staff College and the Joint Services Staff College and entered Parliament in 1954.

Patrick Wall MP

THE WEST AND SOUTH AFRICA

The Energy Crisis

FOR GENERATIONS we in the Free World have taken cheap oil for granted. Our energy policies and manufacturing industries have assumed this premise. Hence the traumatic shock felt by the Western world and Japan at the recent sudden and unilateral action by the Arab States in not only restricting supplies but in demanding higher and higher prices for their oil. This policy was inspired by the Arab/Israeli war of 1973: subsequently it has been applied for reasons wholly unconnected with the dispute with Israel.

It is not only a matter of the effect upon the Western world itself; the effect of higher oil prices on the economies of the countries of the Third World could become catastrophic. Estimates show that the developing countries as a whole will have to face up to a fivefold increase in their total oil import bill. This in turn will have repercussions on the economies of developed nations which could be further affected should some primary producers attempt to emulate the Arabs by withholding their minerals or raw materials in order to force up world prices. The Western world's appetite for oil is enormous. The world's requirements escalated from 539 million tons in 1950 to 1,061 million tons in 1960, 2,276 million tons in 1970 and to an estimated 4,221 million tons in 1980. The U.S. has its own supply of crude oil amounting to about 75.5 per cent of its requirements but reserves are becoming exhausted and imports are rising. In 1973 8.5 per cent came from Canada, 6.5 per cent from the

Middle East, 3.7 per cent from Black Africa, 2.6 per cent from South America, 1 per cent from Iran and lesser quantities from Indonesia and other suppliers. The American position is therefore worrying though not desperate.

Europe, however, is in a much more vulnerable position. Western Europe imports most of its oil from the Middle East, the imports from NATO nations being shown on pages 56 and 57. Gulf oil amounts to some 57 per cent of Europe's imports or about 50 per cent of the total Middle East production, an additional 25 per cent going to Japan which is almost wholly dependent upon the Middle East. Until recently it was thought that while the U.S's imports from the Gulf would greatly increase, Europe's would remain at approximately the present figure, as the new North Sea oilfields would supply the additional requirements for Europe for the forseeable future. Later Arctic oil and new off-shore fields would probably make Europe less reliant on the Middle East but there would be a twenty year energy gap during which both Europe and the U.S. would depend on Middle East oil, most of which would be shipped round the Cape of Good Hope. Recent events in the Middle East have altered this picture. The Arab nations have made it clear that they will not only use oil as a weapon in the war against Israel but will also cut off oil to nations for political reasons unconnected with these recurrent hostilities. An example is the boycott of South Africa and Rhodesia which countries played no part in the Yom Kippur war (1973). This action together with nationalisation of Arab oil and its erratic and escalating price mean that the whole of the industrialised West will now turn its efforts to finding alternative sources of energy and alternative supplies of oil. (Oil will always be required for the petro-chemical industries even if it can be replaced as a fuel.) The "oil gap" during which the West is bound to Middle East supplies may therefore be reduced from twenty to some ten years.

The fact remains that at least until the mid 1980's Middle East oil and the supply routes are of vital importance to the West. This raises two major problems. Can this oil be denied to the West by the producing nations or by other powers, *i.e.* the USSR and her allies, either at the source or by the cutting of the supply routes?

The Arab nations have shown us how far they are prepared to go in reducing oil supplies for political purposes, but their solidarity has already been breached and individual states are making bilateral supply agreements with various European nations. Moreover the Arab nations would suffer too much themselves as they are dependent on the West for manufactured goods. A serious long term cutback in supply is therefore unlikely. Price is going to be their major political weapon and the enormously inflated oil royalties they will receive and invest in the world's money markets make this a very powerful weapon.

What, then, is the danger of the intervention of a third power, namely the USSR, in the Gulf area in the immediate future?

The division of Gulf oil production between a number of states prone to dynastic rivalries provides the Soviet Union, as the nearest major political power, with an opportunity to fill the political/military vacuum which exists in the Gulf following British withdrawal from the area, despite the steps that have been taken to build up Iranian forces, which are now the most powerful in the Gulf. In the present conditions, the possibility of the USSR intervening in any new dynastic dispute between Gulf States, in order to obtain oil or to deny it to others, must be an anxiety to the West, in particular the danger of closing the Persian Gulf, by, for example, the mining of the Straits of Hormuz, thus preventing the exit of oil tankers bound for the U.S. or Europe.

There is of course no need for the Soviet Union to take special political or military action to obtain oil supplies for itself from the Persian Gulf. All the Governments concerned have access to "royalty oil" that they are free to sell to the Soviet Union or Eastern Europe at any time. But as far back as 1921 the Soviet Union restated her oil claims in North Iran and in 1947 she made these a condition of withdrawing her troops from Azerbaijan. Today, the Soviet need for oil from the Middle East is greater than in either 1921 or

Europe's Withdrawal from Africa

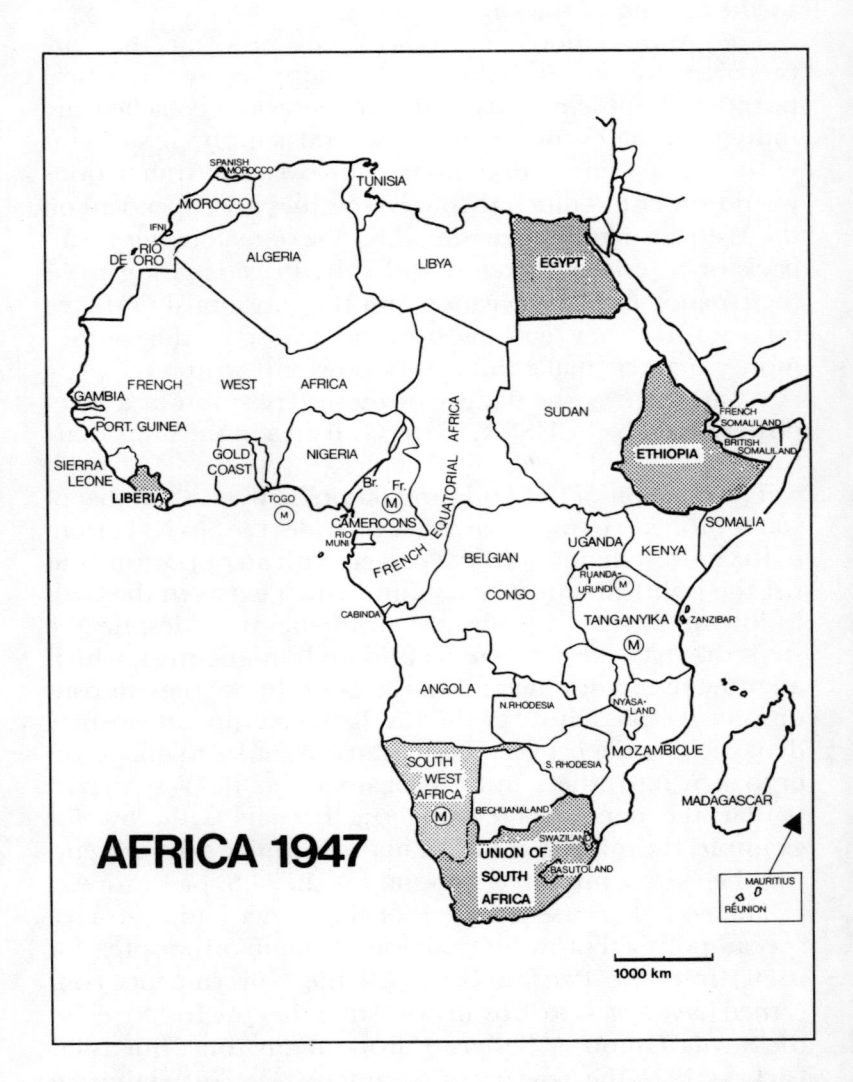

AFRICA 1947

Territories under colonial rule are shown in white, independent countries shaded. M = Mandated territory.

THE WEST AND SOUTH AFRICA

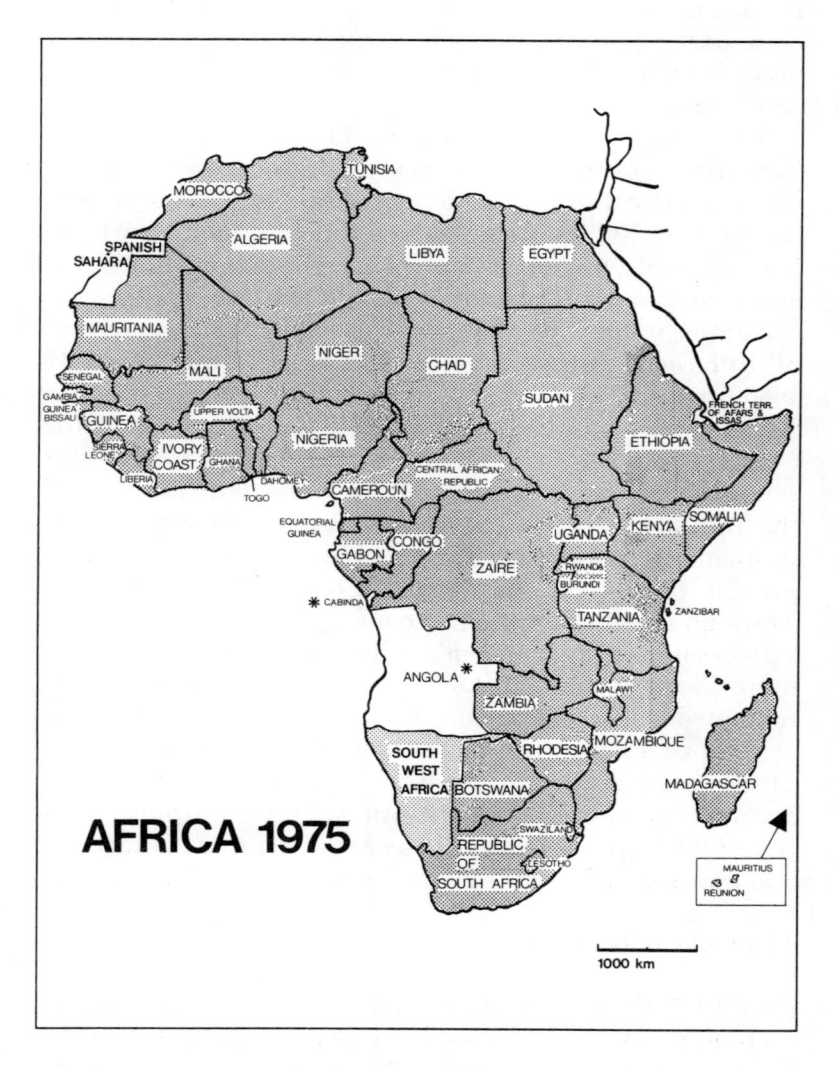

AFRICA 1975

* The progress to independence of Angola was not resolved by early 1975.

1947. Although the USSR is the world's second largest producer (372 million tons in 1971, and production growing at a rate of some 7 per cent per year), she now seems to be close to the point of not being able to satisfy all her own needs from her own resources, let alone supplying the needs of Eastern Europe.

It is expected that the USSR will become an importer of high grade oils during the coming decade, unless she discovers more oil in the Arctic, as she not only has to supply the needs of her industries, which function inefficiently on low grade oils, but retain control over the major deliveries of energy resources to Eastern Europe, where her satellites are becoming restless. In 1969, she exported 25 million tons of oil to Eastern Europe, or some 55% of its requirements. By 1980, this may grow to 140 million tons a year.

The Soviet Union has therefore a direct interest in the Gulf for her own, as yet, comparatively small needs. This can provide a valid excuse to pursue longer term plans to fill the military vacuum left by the British, to step up her influence in such socialist states as Iraq and Syria, to reduce present US interest in Saudi Arabia and to gain direct (through client governments) control of the main source of European and Japanese energy supplies. Such methods are more likely than a military intervention even if this was requested by one of the smaller Arab States, since any intervention in a key area such as the Gulf would run a risk of precipitating a third World War. There are, of course, other alternatives such as the interruption of the oil supply routes round the Cape which would seem to offer more vulnerable and less risky targets; these will be examined in later pages.

The Cold War in Africa

In 1945 there were three African independent nations excluding South Africa — Ethiopia, Egypt and Liberia. Now there are thirty-seven. This rapid change has been caused by the withdrawal of the European colonial powers who introduced modern technology to Africa but left before creating a large enough cadre of those required to govern, administer and control a modern state. The result has been the re-introduction of tensions and rivalries which have been more tribal and internal, rather than external disputes between nations. The struggles that have taken place in recent years include civil wars in Nigeria, the Sudan and the Central African Republic, the protracted revolts and assaults on Tutsi by Hutu in Rwanda and vice versa in Burundi, and the struggle between Eritreans and Amhara in Ethiopia. These are paralleled by local national rivalries in Africa today, for example between Somalia and Ethiopia. As the Arabs can unite in one cause — against Israel — so the Africans can unite in one cause: to "free" the South. That is to say that they can come together to conferences and join in propaganda but they find it difficult to achieve any cohesive or purposeful action.

The desire for liberation and the strategic importance of Southern Africa give the communist powers, the USSR and China, the opportunity not only to strike a blow at the West but at each other. It is significant that each national liberation movement in southern and central Africa has two organisations, one backed and armed by the USSR and the other by China. A study of the achievements of these "liberation movements" is of interest and indicate that their activities rose to a peak between 1962 and 1969 and then declined. A new initiative took place in 1973 and is still continuing especially in Mozambique and to a lesser extent in Rhodesia. Either the Soviet Union or Communist China have backed all the African nationalist organisations mentioned below, with military training and arms. Training has taken place in the USSR and China themselves, and in Tanzania and Algeria under the auspices of one or other of the Communist powers. As a rule, Russian or Chinese influences have been represented in rivalries between organisations competing for support in each of the territories. Let us take each country in turn:-

South Africa In 1912 the ANC (African National Congress) was founded but only became actively involved in direct defiance of the government from 1952 until it was banned in 1960 after Sharpeville. The PAC (Pan-African

Congress) broke away in 1958 and was also banned in 1960. In 1960 both organisations went underground and formed activist wings. The Spear of the Nation (ANC) and Poqo (PAC). Guerilla fighters were trained abroad from about 1962 but Poqo's "Great Revolution" failed in 1963 and many underground leaders were rounded up at Rivonia in the same year. Since then little has been heard of either organisation in South Africa though both have been active abroad. In 1967 ANC combined with ZAPU to invade Rhodesia from Zambia in order to, in the words of their communiqué, "fight their way to strike at the Boers themselves in South Africa". The invasion ended in the Wankie Game Reserve near the Zambian border.

Rhodesia ZAPU (Zimbabwe African People's Union) was formed from the National Democratic Party when this was banned in 1961. ZANU (Zimbabwe African National Union) broke away in 1963. Both established their headquarters in Lusaka, guerillas being trained in China or the USSR and being held in training camps in Zambia. ZANU infiltrated three groups across the Zambesi in 1966, but the first major operation actually took place under ZAPU working in conjunction with the ANC in 1967. At the end of that year five base camps were established inside Rhodesia which were discovered early in 1968 when a major action took place in which ZAPU were defeated. In view of the co-operation of ANC South African armed police came north to assist the Rhodesian Security Forces in patrolling the Zambesi. Two further incursions took place in 1968, one involving the South African police in military action. In it was claimed that 600 trained guerillas were waiting to cross the Zambesi but quarrels between ZAPU and ZANU continued and nothing happened except for two minor incursions in 1970. Tactics have since changed and single men were infiltrated to create cells in the townships. These were of great assistance to Bishop Muzorewa's African National Committee in resisting the Pearce Commission's proposals. ZANU and ZAPU appeared to be willing to merge in Frolizi: today, all three organisations maintain their separate identities and their rivalry.

The lull between 1970 and 1972 ended at Christmas 1972 when guerillas attacked Altena Farm in the Centenary area of North East Rhodesia. Other farms were then attacked and two European land inspectors murdered. The Security Forces discovered that for the first time subversion of the African people had been successful and had been going on for several months. ZANU had been acting in co-operation with FRELIMO and 1973 saw major operations in this area which were still continuing in late 1974 after some 300 guerillas had been killed.

South West Africa SWANU (South West African National Union) consisting mainly of the Herero tribe, was formed in 1960 after the Windhoek riots; SWAPO (South West African People's Union) was organised in the following year largely from among the Ovambo tribe — by far the largest tribe. In 1964 SWAPO sent guerillas to be trained abroad who returned in 1966 and engaged in minor clashes with the South African police. There have been no large scale guerilla activities since, except for minor raids from Zambia into the Caprivi strip, together with considerable laying of anti-personnel mines.

Angola The MPLA (Movemento Popular de Libertação de Angola) was formed in 1956 and the UPA[1] (União das Populacos de Angola) in 1951. In 1961 the MPLA created trouble in Luanda the capital, and in March UPA raised the Bakongo tribe in the North and invaded Angola from the Congo (now Zaire). For a few weeks it was touch and go but in spite of appalling atrocities the Portuguese peasant farmer stayed firm and when the army arrived from Portugal a few months later the North was gradually pacified. In 1965 both organisations attacked Cabinda, a Portuguese enclave north of the River Congo (Zaire), but failed in this comparatively easy task. In 1966 a third organisation, UNITA (National Union for the Total Independence of Angola) initiated attacks from Zambia against the copper carrying Benguela Railway in Eastern Angola. In 1968 they were joined by MPLA and in 1969 by UPA. But this important railway system continues to operate.

1. UPA is now known as FLA.

Mozambique The Portuguese were taken by surprise in Angola in 1961 but they were ready for the rising of the Maconde tribe in Northern Mozambique in 1964. MANU (Mozambique African National Union) initiated the first attack at Nagololo but FRELIMO (Frente de Libertação de Mozambique), formed in 1962, was better organised, strongly supported by Tanzania and had considerable success. Their maximum penetration was achieved in the northern Cabo Delgado district in 1966 and in the adjacent Nyassa district along Lake Malawi in the same year. However, the Portuguese continued to hold all the towns and villages, even those on the frontier, and in a counter-offensive virtually cleared Nyassa district in 1969 and Cabo Delgado in 1970. Meanwhile the FRELIMO leader, Dr Mondlane, was killed by a bomb in Dar-es-Salaam by rival African nationalists, and following his death were a considerable number of desertions and increasing dissension among the leadership. African nationalist attention turned to the Tete district where the Cabora Bassa dam was under construction. The year 1973 saw a major effort by both FRELIMO and COREMO (the successor organisation to MANU) in Tete. They were helped by the fact that many Africans had to be moved from the lake site and re-housed in protected villages, causing considerable disruption of their lives. Groups penetrated beyond Tete, over the Zambesi into the centre of Mozambique in an attempt to spread subversion among local Africans. Traffic on the Umtali-Beira road and railway was frequently interrupted. FRELIMO admitted publicly that the completion of the dam (due in 1976) would undermine their chances of success — presumably because of the vast economic development and raising of local living standards that the dam would bring

In 1974, however, came the collapse of the Caetano government in Lisbon, and the *volte face* in Africa, bringing to power a FRELIMO government in Lourenço Marques — though a peaceful transition to independence appears unlikely due to the traditional rivalry between the Maconde, FRELIMO's ethnic base, and the larger Macua, hitherto pro-Portuguese.

With the Compliments

of the

*Information Service
of South Africa*

655 MADISON AVENUE • NEW YORK, N. Y. 10021 • (212) 838-1700

Race in South Africa

It was against this background and the recurring *coups d'etat*, pogroms and revolutions in independent African states to the North (thirty-nine from 1964 to 1974) that one has to weigh the South African Government's policy of apartheid or separate development.

This concept can be traced from the early development of South Africa and can be dated back to 1652 when white settlement was begun by the Dutch East India Company, slave labour being imported from East and West Africa and the East Indies and the marriage of Europeans with freed slaves of full colour being banned. The British occupied the Cape in 1795 and again in 1806, the next century and a half saw the struggle between Boer and Briton — a period which included the abolition of slavery, the 1820 wave of British settlers, the growth of the missions, the Great Trek of 1838, the Anglo-Boer War and the Act of Union of 1910.

The Boers believed that it was ordained that the African should serve the European and that the relationship between them should therefore be that of servant and master. Indeed, this view was written into the constitution of the old South African Republic, which stated categorically that "the people desire to permit no equality between coloured people and the white inhabitants of the country either in Church or State". This doctrine was preserved by the Treaty of Vereeniging when the British Liberal Government gave self-government to the former Boer Republics of the Transvaal and the Orange Free State; it was later incorporated in the South Africa Act which the British Parliament approved in 1909, the Act of Union excluding non-whites from both Houses of Parliament. The Cape, however, pursued a more liberal policy and it was not until the National Government enlarged the Senate and thus created an artificial two-thirds majority in both Houses sitting together, that they were able to remove the Coloured (mixed race) voters from the Cape voters' roll in 1951.

Apartheid was defined and proclaimed by Dr. D.F. Malan

in 1948. His successor, J.G. Strijdom, determined to carry this policy to its ultimate conclusion, stated in Parliament that the only way in which the white man could maintain his leadership was by domination. "Call it paramountcy, *baaskap* or what you will, it is still domination." This was the apogee of Afrikaner belief and this attitude appeared to be sealed in 1961 when, under the Premiership of Dr. H.F. Verwoerd, South Africa became a Republic and left the Commonwealth.

Since then there has been a gradual shift of emphasis away from the domination factor inherent in the original concept of apartheid towards a policy of separate development. Both the late Dr. Verwoerd and the present premier, B.J. Vorster, have repeatedly indicated that the long term aim of separate development is to create separate but equal freedoms for the various population groups, and have expressly stated that the perpetuation of domination of one group by another could not but end in chaos for all concerned. Although the merits of this policy and the government's ability, means and total commitment to face the ultimate consequences of this policy may be questioned, the shift away from domination as the cornerstone of Afrikaner policy represents a fundamental change which the rest of the world has largely failed to appreciate. This lack of perception has been subsequently reflected in the reaction of most of the country's enemies and critics alike and is one of the reasons why their comments and arguments have had so little impact on political opinion within South Africa.

South Africa's racial problem is particularly intricate for two reasons. First, because of the high proportion of Whites 1:3¼ compared with Africans who are grouped in eight main nations or 1:2¼ if Coloured (mixed race) are included among the Whites. Secondly because South Africa is a modern industrialised society where the technical knowledge and skill of the white man and his power to attract capital is at present as important, or even more important, than the labour and growing skill of the black man which as he progresses will gain him increasing economic and therefore political power.

What of the future? Can a multi-racial society be created out of the two white groups, Afrikaans and English speaking, the Coloured, the Indian and the several Bantu nations with their ten different languages? Dr. H. Muller, South Africa's foreign minister, thinks not and concludes: "All the evidence so far clearly suggests that where both Black and White communities are substantial and permanent in Africa there is essentially only a struggle for power — for supremacy — between them."

Is there therefore to be a continuous and growing struggle? Many in Europe and the U.S. would answer yes but most South Africans believe that there is an alternative — separate development, its aim being the creation of viable and autonomous Bantu nations alongside and in association with the white nation and the Indian community; a South African commonwealth of peoples. The first "homeland" to achieve independence as a separate, self-governed and economically viable nation is likely to be the Xhosa territory of the Transkei — a development that may be expected by the end of the present decade.

Nowhere in the world has a comparable problem yet been solved. It is a matter that will, however, have to be settled by the people of Southern Africa and not by outside intervention. Some prophesy revolution but evolution seems far more probable, and only evolution can bring peace and prosperity to the people of all races.

The Threat to the West

Even when the Suez Canal is re-opened the Cape Route will remain a vital highway for the West's supply of oil, raw materials and food. The majority of the world's population and much of its raw materials lie in the area around the Indian Ocean and South Pacific. The world's centre of gravity has shifted to this region at a time when the Western Powers have almost completed their withdrawal, the British from the Persian Gulf and the Americans from Vietnam. Even the future of the Commonwealth force in Singapore is now uncertain due to the action of the new Labour Government in Australia and the commitment of the new Labour Government in Britain to cut defence spending. Simultaneously Soviet influence is increasing throughout the area and Chinese influence is spreading in South East Asia. Small nations no longer look to the West to protect them. As yet they may well be too weak to stand on their own feet and may therefore bow to Communist economic and military pressure. Alliances such as ANZUS, SEATO and CENTO have lost much of their appeal when the key Western nations give the appearance of having lost their will to help their friends and spend too much time quarrelling among themselves.

Meanwhile Soviet maritime power increases throughout the area. Not only will they virtually control the Suez Canal when it is re-opened, but they now have close links with countries such as the Somali Republic and South Yemen, from where they could seal off the Red Sea, as well as with the major states such as India and Bangladesh. The vast majority of the world's trade is still carried by sea, where the submarine is the major threat. Even in the Second World War the German U-boats caused havoc with allied shipping round the Cape and in the Madagascar Channel. Germany started that war with a fleet of some sixty submarines, today the USSR has over one hundred nuclear powered submarines, more than all the NATO fleets together and is building at the rate of at least 15 a year. Some eighty of these vessels are missile submarines and some thirty attack submarines: they are backed by a large fleet of conventional submarines. At the start of the Battle of the Atlantic the ratio of German submarines to Allied anti-submarine vessels was 1:5·9; today the ratio of Soviet submarines to NATO anti-submarine vessels is 1:1·6.

In 1949 NATO's southern boundary was set at the Tropic of Cancer (north of the Equator), at that time the limit of a conventional Soviet submarine's range. Today's nuclear submarine can travel round the world without surfacing, making it much less vulnerable to surface vessels or aircraft.

In spite of the fact that over 1,000 ships a month use South African ports and some sixty per cent are bound to or from Western Europe, the West has as yet no positive policy for protecting their shipping in the Indian Ocean or in the South Atlantic. The main reason is that Western politicians do not wish to be seen associating with South Africa because of the political unpopularity of the policy of apartheid. South African and (if still usable) Portuguese African ports would, however, play a vital role in the defence of shipping in time of tension. Not only can South Africa, Mozambique and Angola provide ports and airfields but they are backed by the largest industrial complex in the Southern Hemisphere. Drydocks and repair facilities exist at a number of ports. South African yards now build ships of up to 8,000 tons. Aviation and electronic repairs can be carried out and many subsidiaries linked to major European industrial firms are involved in the operations. Heavy industries are backed by reserves of raw material and food and the country provides an excellent climate for rest and recuperation.

However, the only direct bond with the West is through the Anglo-South African Simonstown Agreement which has been maintained by both Conservative and Labour Governments in Britain. This Agreement was signed in 1955 and includes a Sea Routes Agreement which states "Recognising the importance of sea communications to the well being of their respective countries in peace and to their common security in event of aggression, the Governments of the Union of South Africa and of the United Kingdom enter into the following Agreement to ensure the safety, by joint operations of their maritime forces, of the sea routes round Southern Africa." This Agreement gave Britain many advantages, including the use of Simonstown in peace and war and facilities at other ports (but not airfields) even when South Africa was not at war. If both countries were involved in war the British Commander-in-Chief was to have operational command. In return Britain agreed to re-equip the South African Navy. In 1967 the British Labour Government re-negotiated the Simonstown Agreement, the main provisions being left unchanged but the British C-in-C

South Atlantic was withdrawn and replaced by a Commodore as the Royal Navy's representative, the South African Navy assuming a greater responsibility for the area[1].

Since the late 1960's the Soviet Navy has become an oceanic power and not only are NATO's sea flanks in the Arctic and in the Mediterranean threatened but NATO's backdoor at the Cape becomes even more vulnerable. In 1971 the North Atlantic Assembly set up a committee to study the Soviet maritime threat. This committee reported at the meeting in Bonn in November 1972 and recommended that NATO's Supreme Allied command Atlantic (SACLANT) be given the authority to plan for the Indian Ocean and the South Atlantic, including surveillance and communications. This report was approved and passed on to the NATO Council for implementation.

SACLANT has its headquarters at Norfold, Virginia. Shipping entering European waters from the South Atlantic would in war be controlled from the IBERLANT headquarters near Lisbon. Though good communications exist between the Royal Navy and the South African Navy, what is needed is direct communications with other NATO headquarters as well as realistic maritime exercises with NATO forces and merchant shipping. The South African Navy is an effective anti-submarine force but requires both modernisation and expansion, both of which are checked by the political attitude of the United Nations and some of its members. Portugal is, at the time of writing, a member of NATO, and her ports, particularly the Cape Verde Islands, Luanda, Lourenço Marques and Beira with their associated airfields would be of great importance. But Portugal's authority will have ended in Lourenço Marques and Beira by 1975, and most probably in Luanda soon after.

Specially equipped aircraft such as the RAF's long range "Nimrod" and seaborne helicopters are today the most effective anti-submarine weapon systems. To operate these aircraft in the South Atlantic and Indian Oceans requires the use of airfields and an adequate number of frigates from which anti-submarine helicopters can operate. Thus South African, Portuguese and Rhodesian airfields are of primary

---

[1]. In December 1974 the British Labour Government announced their decision to abrogate the Simonstown Agreement.

importance. As far as the RAF is concerned these facilities are currently available only at Masira (off the coast of Oman) and at Gan, though Mauritius and the Seychelles now have good commercial airfields. Agreement was reached between the last British Conservative Government (1970-74) and the U.S. Government to enlarge the present communications centre on the British island of Diego Garcia and to provide a military airfield and supply facilities. This agreement may not be so enthusiastically supported by the present British Labour Government and has run into difficulty in the U.S. Senate on the grounds of cost. The Diego Garcia project may turn out to be even more important from a political than from a military point of view. Indian Ocean countries backed by India have initiated a resolution in the United Nations General Assembly which was passed by a large majority demanding a neutralisation of that ocean. As usual the wrath of these professional neutrals is directed more against the West than against the USSR or China. If the West were now to abandon Diego Garcia, their interpretation would be that the West was indeed abandoning that ocean to the domination of Soviet maritime power.

The Soviet fleet first appeared in the Mediterranean in 1964, and was established on a permanent basis by 1967. This fleet considerably increased the sphere of Soviet influence particularly in the Arab world. This tactic is now being repeated in the Indian Ocean. Figures of ship/days of Soviet warships and auxiliaries (excluding submarines) show an alarming increase:-

1969	1,400
1970	2,450
1971	2,250
1972	5,200
1973	7,250

Soon the USSR will be able to use the Suez Canal to switch her main fleet from the Mediterranean to the Indian Ocean. Already she has a number of anchorages and use of base

1970 CRUDE OIL IMPORTS BY EUROPEAN

From \ To	NORWAY	DENMARK	NETHERLANDS	BELGIUM	UNITED KINGDOM	PORTUGAL
CARIBBEAN	1.22	0.37	1.21	2.85	5.15	—
WEST AFRICA	1.11	1.81	7.72	0.73	7.61	0.11
OTHER AFRICA	—	—	1.33	0.23	0.51	—
ALGERIA	0.05	0.11	0.25	1.54	1.32	—
LIBYA	0.60	1.28	12.17	6.09	23.73	—
EGYPT	—	0.21	0.38	0.23	0.32	—
IRAQ (3)(5)	—	—	5.05	1.09	2.40	2.03
SAUDI ARABIA (4)(5)	1.07	1.41	9.23	5.08	16.08	0.64
KUWAIT (5)	0.68	2.84	11.63	5.24	26.11	—
IRAN (5)	0.22	0.65	6.08	3.50	8.43	0.12
OTHER MIDDLE EAST	1.58	1.28	3.49	2.67	8.15	0.79
BLACK SEA	—	—	—	0.50	—	—
TOTAL	6.53	9.96	58.31	29.75	99.81	3.69

Notes:

(1) Source O.E.C.D.
(2) Ministry of Trade and Industry, London, estimates entry of French and German is divided as follows:

	Atlantic Ports	Mediterranean Ports
FRANCE	58.6	42.7
GERMANY	56.7	42.1

(3) Ministry of Trade and Industry also estimates that 10.4 million tons of Iraq's oil is routed via the Cape of Good Hope, the remaining 43.1 million tons is piped to Mediterranean terminals.

NATO NATIONS (1) Unit: 000,000 Metric Tons

WEST GERMANY (2)	FRANCE (2)	ITALY	GREECE	TURKEY	TOTAL	ATLANTIC AND NORTH SEA PORTS (2) (5)	MED PORTS (2) (5)
3.40	2.45	2.21	—	—	18.86	16.65	2.21
6.95	6.85	0.54	—	—	33.43	36.41	0.54
0.99	0.46	—	—	—	3.52		
7.98	26.99	2.84	0.1	0.03	41.21		
40.92	17.64	35.62	0.3	0.49	138.84		
1.27	0.62	1.52	—	—	4.55	85.01	153.15
3.48	12.16	21.58	2.9	2.87	53.56		
12.06	9.45	16.28	0.6	0.41	72.31		
3.95	11.09	13.82	—	—	75.36		
8.27	3.79	6.36	—	—	37.42	180.07	41.87
6.07	8.42	4.35	—	0.05	36.85		
3.44	1.42	8.83	0.6	—	14.79	0.50	14.29
98.78	101.34	113.94	4.60	3.85	530.72	318.64	212.06

(4) The same source estimates 9 million tons of Saudi Arabian oil was piped to the Mediterranean. The Tapline was closed from May 1970.
(5) Oil from these countries is routed via the Cape. Total 223,500,000 tons, including Iraqi oil.
(6) Entry into Med/Atlantic ports is calculated on the assumption that oil for France and Germany imported through Mediterranean ports is supplied from the Black Sea and Mediterranean terminals only. (i.e., oil for these countries from Caribbean, African and Gulf Ports is imported via Atlantic ports, as is the surplus from the Mediterranean terminals).
(7) Sources of Greek imports estimated to be proportional to 1969 figure.

ports in India, Sri Lanka, the Somali Republic and South Yemen (Aden), as well as a long range aircraft base and naval squadron in Conakry in Guinea. In fact, the position in this area is becoming exactly the opposite of that in the Second World War when the Allied navies controlled all major ports and airfields and were eventually able to check and repulse Japanese penetration.

Many South Africans have taken the view that the two Communist giants, the USSR and China, are gradually implementing a policy that will cut the continent of Africa in half from Zanzibar to Brazzaville and that later, when this penetration has been completed, will launch attacks on the South from this belt of satellite or friendly countries. They point to the 30,000 Chinese Communist "soldiers" building the Tan-Zam railway, the assistance given to the "freedom fighters" and the continued subversion of the continent which the West does nothing to check. Should this happen the West would be forced to react, as the concept of an "unaligned" South Africa or an anti-West South Africa would be too dangerous to contemplate. Such reaction could come so late as to run the risk of a direct confrontation with one or both of the Communist giants.

From the Soviet point of view it would be less costly in treasure and lives to cut the sea routes round the Cape and effectively starve NATO of oil. Under present circumstances the only response could be nuclear war or surrender, because NATO is today too weak and too unprepared to offer effective conventional resistance. The USSR could therefore decide to use the technique of blackmail during the next few years when Soviet maritime power reaches its peak in relation to the West. Unless the West is prepared to react, such blackmail could be only too effective. Truly, the Cape is NATO's backdoor which has been left virtually unguarded: it is high time that we in the West wake up to this fact. The real need is for a joint defence agreement between the industrialised countries of the Southern Hemisphere backed by adequate Western sea/air power.

The importance of South Africa

South Africa is the world's largest supplier of the world's most precious metal, gold, and its most precious stone, the diamond. For centuries men have fought over these exotic minerals. Today modern technology has given enhanced importance to such minerals as uranium, chrome and vanadium, all of which are found in large quantities in the Republic of South Africa. Exports of these materials to the West are of great strategic and economic importance. As far as food is concerned South Africa is virtually self-supporting and exports maize, sugar, tobacco and fruit as well as wood, karakul, mohair and hides. In fact, South Africa has everything she wants except oil for which widespread prospecting both onshore and offshore is now being carried out. At the time of the crisis with the U.N. over South West Africa in 1966, the government is said to have stockpiled two to three years' supply.

South Africa is one of the world's leading trading nations. In 1971 total exports, excluding gold, were valued at R1,568.8 (£1 = $1.6, $1 = R.7) million and total imports at R.887.0 million, the balance being more than made up by gold exports. The value of exports by continents in 1971 were as follows:-

Europe	R776.8 millions
America	170.2
Africa	292.4
Asia	233.9
Oceania	16.2

Imports in the same year were:-

Europe	R1,572.5 millions
America	541.4
Africa	127.4
Asia	542.3
Oceania	74.2

As far as Great Britain and the U.S. were concerned the figures were as follows:

G.B. Exports to: R.418.8 m Imports from: R.669.8 m
U.S.A. Exports to: 121.1 Imports from: 469.3

These figures emphasise the Republic's economic attachment to the West, over half of her exports and imports going to or coming from Europe, and some 7 per cent of her exports and 16 per cent of her imports to or from the U.S.

They also illustrate why investment in South Africa from overseas has continued for so many years and has brought such a good return, the average being 14 per cent, one of the highest in the world. Total foreign investment in 1970 was R.5,818 m and net inflow was R541 m. The Sterling Area has the major share, some R3,371 m or about 58 per cent, and the Dollar Area about 18 per cent.

It is sometimes argued that for political reasons Britain would do better to increase her investment in Black Africa and decrease her stake in South Africa. A comparison of figures in 1973 quoted in the House of Commons was:-

	Black Africa	Southern Africa
Book value of investment less oil	£352 m	£740 m
Oil investment	£150 to £200 m	—
Holding of securities	—	£1,000 m
1972 imports from	£457 inc. oil	£352 m
1972 exports from	£405 m	£342 m

Investments are therefore heavily in favour of the South while trade is slightly in favour of the North but this must be balanced against the security of British trade and investment in the South and the growing practice of nationalisation and expropriation in the North.

South Africa is therefore not only the most industrialised area and the country with the strongest economy in Africa, but also in the Southern Hemisphere; hence the growing importance of links with such countries as the Argentine and Brazil and also with Australia and New Zealand. Unfortunately, the advent of left-wing governments in Australia and New Zealand have checked any further developments for the time being. Nothing can, however, check the importance of the Cape of Good Hope as one of the world's major communications centres, lying as it does in the centre of the southern oceans. This importance has been enhanced since the closure of the Suez Canal but will remain even when the Canal is re-opened, not least because modern tanker fleets are composed of ships too large for the Canal.

The Cape route is now the most crowded shipping lane in the world. Over half of Europe's oil supplies and a quarter of its food come round the Cape of Good Hope and through the South Atlantic. Different sources estimate that by 1975 between forty and sixty per cent of the U.S.'s oil requirements will also be supplied by this route.

The number of ships which called at South African ports each year is as follows:-

1957/58	6,300	1965/66	7,941
1958/59	6,360	1966/67	8,111
1959/60	6,051	1967/68	12,701
1960/61	6.256	1968/69	12,275
1961/62	6,352	1969/70	12,315
1962/63	6,546	1970/71	12,528
1963/64	6,970	1971/72	12,021
1964/65	7,468	1972/73	11,469

The problem of defending vital shipping in time of war is immense. Recent events have at least brought to the notice of the general public the West's present dependence on Middle Eastern oil.

In February 1972, the following NATO ships passed the Cape of Good Hope:

British	257 freighters	112 tankers	Total 369	or 20.1 %
(Liberian)(US)	90	182	272	14.82
Norwegian	79	125	204	11.12
Greek	61	28	89	4.89
Netherlands	58	25	83	4.52
French	43	39	82	4.47
West German	52	16	68	3.72
Italian	43	20	63	3.43
Danish	30	14	44	2.41
American	35	3	38	2.07
Portuguese	18	5	23	1.25
NATO (total)	476	387	1,063	57.99
South Africa	21	0	21	1.14
Grand Total all shipping	1,132	703	1,835	

The total capacity of these 1,835 ships is approximately:

Freighters	11,320,000 GRT	(all laden)
Tankers	28,120,000 DWT	(½ in ballast)

In June 1972, 1,030 ocean going ships called at South African ports. In the same month, 184 Eastern block ships passed the Cape of Good Hope (145 freighters and 39 tankers). In addition, 58 Soviet fishing vessels and support ships were sighted off South-West Africa. It is estimated that 11,000 to 14,000 ships pass the Cape of Good Hope per year without calling at South African ports. The grand total of all ships of all nations passing the Cape of Good Hope thus comes to approximately 24,000 ocean-going ships a year, or 66 per day.

Today neither the Royal Navy nor the U.S. Navy rules the waves. The USSR has the second largest and most modern fleet which includes more nuclear submarines than the U.S., British and French navies put together. This is backed

THE WEST AND SOUTH AFRICA

Soviet and Chinese Diplomatic Presence in Africa, 1975

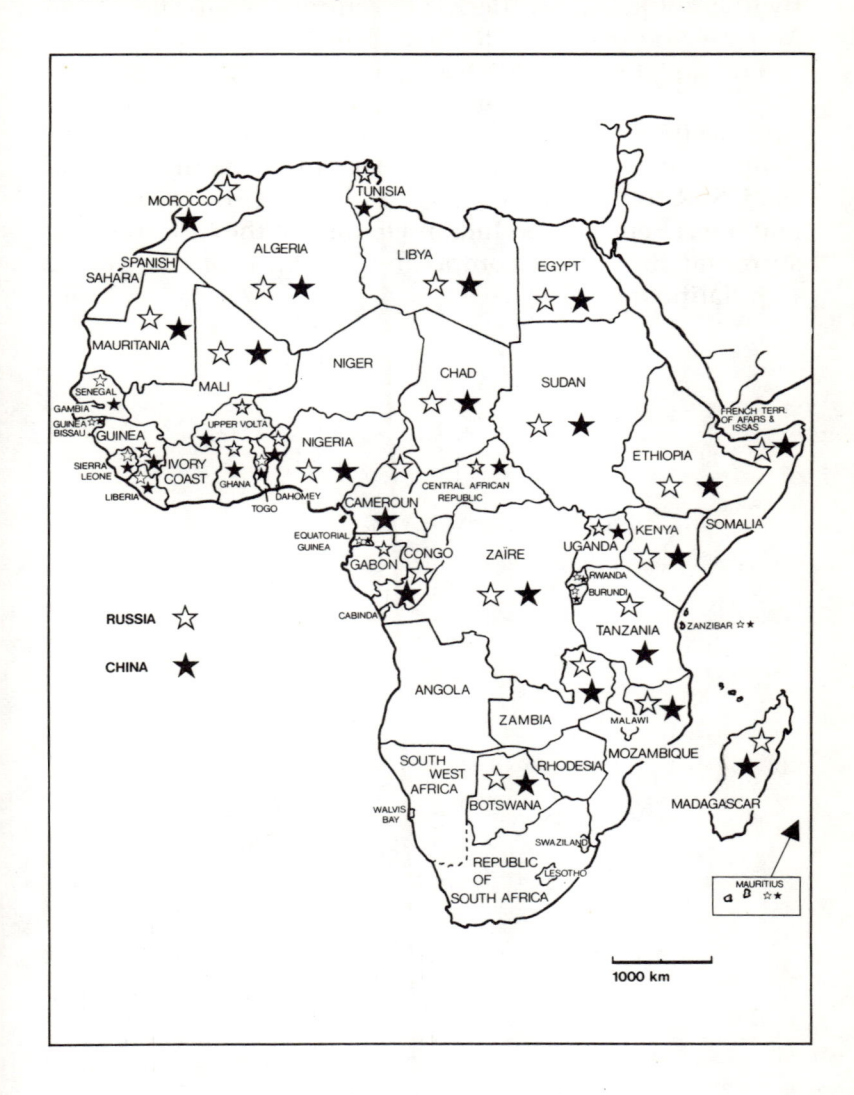

Up until 1957, the only Communist Power representation anywhere in Africa was the USSR's embassy in South Africa.

by a growing merchant marine and the largest fishing and hydrographic survey fleet, all centrally controlled from Moscow and thus all interdependent.

The threat that such a fleet, particularly the submarines, can pose to the West's long and vulnerable route round the Cape route must be obvious. In fact it is so obvious that the danger is not so much the outbreak of war but the power of the USSR to blackmail the West to accept Soviet influence and interference in the Indian Ocean and the countries that surround this ocean comprising the bulk of the world's population.

The Institute for the Study of Conflict has its headquarters in London, at 17 Northumberland Avenue, W C 2. It is headed by Brian Crozier.

Institute for the Study of Conflict

THE SECURITY OF THE CAPE OIL ROUTE

1.

THE FOURTH Arab-Israeli war, and the oil crisis that followed, brought a new awareness of industrial dependence upon an insecure supply of energy. Against the background of this dependence, this ISC Special Report looks at the problems of security in the supply of oil, with special reference to the Cape Route, but without neglecting the producing countries.

More specifically, this report does not deal with the Mediterranean; it is confined to that large portion of Middle East oil that is shipped from the Persian Gulf to Europe and the Western Hemisphere by the Cape Route, and our concern is with all factors that may affect this traffic, not only at present, but for as long as it remains an essential part of the oil requirements of consumers in Europe and America. (It may be that as a result of recent events an intensified search for new sources of oil, and crash programmes aimed at developing alternative sources of energy, will reduce this period, but the "lead times" will cover many years and it seems extremely unlikely that the period of absolute dependence on Middle East oil can be much shorter.)

As we shall show, the problem is not that of being allowed by the Arabs to revert to the level of flow which obtained before the slow-down, but of how far the producer States will be prepared to increase production to meet the constantly growing demands of the Western consumers, whose economies have been geared to expect by 1985 well over twice the amount of Middle East oil they now receive.

There are sound economic reasons why certain producer States may not wish to satisfy the whole of the increase in demand, so that if and when the political restrictions on the flow of oil are lifted we should expect the rate of growth of the oil supply to be somewhat less than many experts have calculated. This would affect the volume of Cape Route traffic, and so would the pending re-opening of the Suez Canal and the construction in Egypt of a pipeline from the Gulf of Suez to the Mediterranean (SUMED) and other pipelines. Nevertheless, even if the growth rate of oil production is to be permanently reduced, and if part of the tanker traffic — and it is unlikely to be a large part — is diverted to the Red Sea we shall give reasons for thinking that the tanker traffic on the Cape Route will increase and continue to be of vital importance to Western economy. (It must also be borne in mind that any future re-closure of the Canal or drastic interference with the pipelines to the Mediterranean would lead to an immediate increase in Cape Route traffic.)

It is therefore essential that this traffic should not be impeded by extraneous factors such as conflict in the Gulf or by interference with the tankers on their way to their destinations. A tanker leaving the head of the Gulf sails past Bahrein and Qatar then between Iran and the Arab Emirates, out through the Straits of Hormuz, along part of the Oman coast, then straight across the Indian Ocean, nearing land opposite Nacala, in Mozambique. Then it follows the African coast to the Cape of Good Hope and strikes out into the Atlantic, either westwards for the Americas, or north-west to skirt the bulge of equatorial Africa before edging eastwards towards the European ports.

There are certain potential risks to the oil traffic along the way, and we shall look at these chiefly in the context of the oil States themselves, and of the littoral States of Southern Africa. Normally, between leaving the Gulf terminal and arriving at its European or American destination, a tanker will make few ports of call, and a very large one none at all. But smaller tankers require bunkering and victualling, and both small and large are occasionally in need of repair, servicing and special facilities. Every day over a million tons of crude oil pass the Cape, heading for the Atlantic. This may be contained in as many as a dozen ships, with a similar number passing in the opposite direction empty, some of which may prefer to make use of the cheaper bunkering facilites at Cape Town. But Cape Town is only one of the ports offering services to the tanker-trade.

One has only to look at the number and size of the tankers awaiting attention outside Lisnave (Lisbon). Cape Verde, Cape Town, Durban and Lourenço Marques and Nacala to realise that tanker servicing in Southern Africa is a big business, and in fact much European capital is being invested in this way. At the Gulf end both Bahrein and Dubai are constructing large dry-docks capable of repairing VLCCs (Very Large Crude Carriers — super tankers of 160,000 tons or more). At present, and for the foreseeable future, all these ports are essential to the tanker traffic, and we shall therefore look at them individually in the light of local conditions that may affect their future as safe havens in which expensive ships may seek the services they need.

Consideration must also be given to the possibility, however remote, of interference with the tanker traffic at sea. In this context the increased presence of the USSR in the Indian Ocean has caused alarm, since it could, in theory, enable the Soviet Navy to seal off the Persian Gulf and halt the whole of the oil flow. In peacetime this is inconceivable; in near-war conditions, or even in a situation of advanced international confrontation, it cannot be excluded. Shore-based intervention by anti-Western revolutionary movements is another possiblity, and here we must look at the stability of the littoral States along the route, that is, in the Gulf, Oman, Southern Africa and western equatorial Africa, and the nature of certain extremist movements.

Although at the time of writing the supply of oil and the approaching energy crisis appear to overshadow everything else, account must be taken of other major factors which may affect the security of the Route: the continuing struggle of the Communist powers to obtain supremacy over the capitalist world, and the bitter conflict between Moscow and Peking to determine which brand of communism shall prevail. There is therefore inserted after Part 2 — *The Economic and Technical Background* — a section, Part 3, which discusses Soviet and Chinese policies in general. Part 4 defines more closely revolutionary and political challenges in the Gulf area; Part 5, security problems in the Gulf oil-producing countries; Part 6, revolutionary and political challenges in the Southern African area, and Part 7, security in Southern Africa. Part 8 seeks to review all the potential threats to the oil route, and discusses what can be done to eliminate them.

It should perhaps be emphasized that a report of this kind, attempting to plot a course through a decade or more of what may prove to be very eventful history, must include an element of contingency thinking. We should not assume too readily that certain things must, or cannot, happen. Looking back, the wisdom of the British decision in 1968 to withdraw from the Gulf is open to doubt, since the elements which created the current situation were all present, and might have been clearly discernible. But looking back is easier than looking forward, which is what this report sets out to do.

2. The Economic and Technical Background

Even before the beginning of the Middle East War of October 1973 statistics of oil reserves, production, delivery and consumption were often inaccurate and sometimes misleading for the layman. As Geoffrey Chandler, President of the Institute of Petroleum, wrote in his Summer Address to the Institute (7 June, 1973): "... no energy paper would be complete without an eyebrow lifted at the grosser infelicities of earlier forecasters". But there are reasons for the inaccuracies. The way in which companies calculate "published proved" figures is based on extreme caution because, obviously, they cannot know what may go wrong when they come to exploit the reserves.

The difficulties inherent in oil statistics apply especially to production and delivery statistics. It is easy to fall into the trap of equating "production level" with "exportable surplus", that is, the volume of oil left for export after a portion has been used for domestic purposes and for the local petrochemical and other industries. Some crudes have a high sulphur content and need expensive processing, before shipment or in the consumer country. Consumers have their special requirements. They may want a mix of various qualities. In fact, the whole of the petroleum industry works on very specific requirements, which explains why the readjustment in consumer countries made necessary by Arab restrictions, is a highly complicated business. Exports of oil cannot easily be switched from one country to another.

Forecasters of oil consumption have consistently underestimated, and at the present moment are likely to be more than ever unreliable, because consumer demand will be affected by economy measures, the effects of the swingeing price-increases and the use of alternative sources of energy. If we accept that even the best available statistics (e.g. Mr. Chandler's in *Appendix II*) are prone to error, we must view any figures put forward in this report with equal caution, and use them to give only a general idea of relative values.

To form an opinion, however speculative, about the future of the Cape oil route we must consider briefly the whole question of supply. James E. Akins, the State Department expert and recently appointed United States Ambassador to Saudi Arabia, wrote last spring (*Foreign Affairs*, April 1973): "... it is agreed on all sides that there is no question of a physical shortage of oil in the world, up to 1980 or 1985, at costs of production comparable to today's". In fact, even if world demand, exclusive of the USSR and the Chinese People's Republic (CPR), rises by 1980 to 85 mbd — more than twice the 1970 figure — there would still remain adequate proved reserves for a further 10 years at the 1980 demand level. But the figure of 85 mbd is a daunting one, in present circumstances, and it is extremely difficult to estimate how far economies and other measures may succeed in reducing it.

On the basis of estimated reserves and current production the non-Arab world, including Iran, might deliver half what is required by 1980, leaving the Arab States to produce the remaining, say, 40 mbd. This will be possible only if the Arab States are willing not only to waive their political objections to supplying certain countries, but to increase their production from 17 mbd in 1973 to 40 mbd in 1980. They appear technically capable of doing this, but there are economic reasons why the wealthier States should not.

Let us examine the case of Saudi Arabia, since it is the only producer able to fill the ultimate gap between production and demand. Before the Middle East war began, an American expert calculated, on the basis of the prices then obtaining, that however much Saudi Arabia might spend on internal development — and he suggested a maximum figure of 16,000 million dollars — it would be left with reserves of 100,000 million dollars in the 1980s — more than the contents of Fort Knox. It may indeed be quite immaterial to King Faisal, from the financial point of view, whether or not to level off production at 10 mbd, which might be his chosen "economic level". The price rises which accompanied the restriction in oil supplies would allow the previously expected level of profit to be maintained, and he would have the further advantage of conserving oil reserves.

In fact — and this point was constantly made by Saudi officials to the *rapporteur* of this Study Group during his visit to their country in early October — the Ruler was prepared to continue the high growth rate of oil production only "as a favour to the West", and on certain conditions, which included not only a radical change in the US attitude to the Arab-Israeli question, but also massive assistance from Western industrialists and technologists to Saudi Arabia so as to transform the country into a modern State.

It is, in fact, quite true that for certain of the producer States it would be more economic to leave part of their oil in the ground, and it is important to understand that many months before the start of the Middle East war Saudi Arabia was playing hard to get, Kuwait had cut back production to 3 mbd (whereas its installations could produce well over 4 mbd), and Abu Dhabi, whose production from existing wells was increasing rapidly, had begun to restrict expansion. This was the situation that so alarmed

Ambassador Akins, who pointed out that the loss of the production of *any one* of these countries could cause a temporary but significant world shortage.

To explain the knife-edge position of oil supply and demand we must look in more detail at the figures. A forecast of the demand for Middle East oil appears in *Appendix III*. Taking 1980 as a date before which it is highly unlikely that new sources of energy or non-Arab oil will be making a substantial contribution to Western economies, it is at once obvious that Europe, requiring 12.8 mbd now, and 19 mbd in 1980, simply cannot afford to lose the goodwill of the Middle East suppliers. Nevertheless, although the forecast increase in consumption is 50 per cent, it may be possible, with economies and with the accelerated exploitation of North Sea reserves and other measures, to keep the annual increase in European demand to a fairly low figure, if this is necessary.

The United States position is quite different. Its current demand from all Middle East sources is small (only 3.3 mbd) which is why it might survive a protracted cut-off without disaster, whereas Europe or Japan obviously could not. But the estimate given for US demand for Middle East oil in 1980 shows an increase of 300 per cent in the six years, from 3.3 to 14 mbd, that is from 20 per cent to 35 per cent of total US consumption. Thus, even taking into account economies and other measures which might alleviate the situation, it seems clear that the United States will require not only the resumption of the oil traffic but a considerable annual increase. Whether they can get it depends essentially on Saudi Arabia.

The chart at *Appendix III* shows that total US, European and Japanese demands for Middle East oil in 1980 will be 42 mbd, while *Appendix II* shows that the Middle East countries, excluding Saudi Arabia might be producing 25.5 mbd in 1980. It follows that Saudi Arabia will have to be producing at the rate of 16.5 mbd if world demands are to be met. But what chance is there that Saudi Arabia will agree to allow production to reach this figure, or even that other States will develop their production as shown in the chart?

The oil-producing States in the Persian Gulf can be broadly divided as follows: Iran (5.8 mbd) and Iraq's case not wholly explored — and great absorptive capacity for the revenue as their governments can usefully spend anything they can earn from oil. Kuwait (3 mbd), Qatar (0.5 mbd), Oman (0.3 mbd) and Dubai (0.3 mbd) have limited reserves and small absorptive capacity, but the two last named — for reasons which will appear later — can absorb their comparatively small revenues. Saudi Arabia (8 mbd) and Abu Dhabi (12 mbd) have large reserves and relatively small absorptive capacity, unless very large new development programmes are put in hand.

In the aftermath of the 1973 Middle East war the situation is broadly as follows:

Iran. Not involved, and has no reason to restrict production.

Iraq. Is involved, but has decided, in view of her urgent need of revenue, to continue to expand production.

Saudi Arabia. Is involved, but will wish to resume expansion at a lower rate, as soon as the political situation allows.

Kuwait and Qatar. Are involved, Qatar might follow Saudi Arabia's lead. Kuwait is taking an independent line.

Abu Dhabi, Dubai, members of the United Arab Emirates (UAE). Are involved, but probably wish to resume full production as soon as possible, perhaps at a slower rate of increase.

Oman. Is involved, and has so far followed Saudi Arabia's lead, but will wish to take the first opportunity of expanding production to maximum economic extent.

It appears likely that if Saudi Arabia decides, after a settlement of the Arab-Israeli situation, to resume production at a lower rate of growth, Abu Dhabi and Dubai would follow suit. Kuwait and Qatar would resume their constant levels of production, and only Iran, Iraq and Oman would wish to expand freely. We thus return again to the key position of Saudi oil policy. If the Saudis decide to slow down the growth-rate beyond the critical limit, no combination of other Gulf States will make up the difference, and the West and Japan will suffer seriously. It can be argued that this is not what Saudi Arabia wants. Traditionally, she has been a friend of the West and totally opposed to Communist influence. But it must be realised that all the rich oil States have suffered from seeing their investments abroad falling in value. The successive devaluations of the dollar and the pound have never been forgiven. The problem of investing what remains of oil revenues after everything possible has been spent on domestic development and "downstream" activities — refineries, tankers, etc. — is still a nightmare to the rulers, who have the rich man's horror of any form of financial loss. If the consumer countries wish to be assured of the growth-rate they require from the Gulf producers, they must produce some solution to this problem. That is, they must be able to show convincingly that it is not more profitable to leave the oil in the ground.

One suggestion made to the *rapporteur* was that oil prices should be linked to the price of gold, which for this purpose should be given, by international agreement, a fixed threshold. Then, if further inflation occurred, the value of oil would rise with the value of gold, but it could never fall below the threshold price. In addition, there would have to be some international machinery for investing surplus oil revenues, with full guarantees to protect the invested capital. It has also been suggested, notably by the Shah of Iran, that oil prices could be linked to the cost of energy or manufactured goods.

This is a problem which extends far beyond the scope of this study. The point we wish to make is that for the reasons given above some such solution must be found if the growth-rate required by the West is to be made acceptable to Saudi Arabia. The alternative is to fall back on a system of oil-price increases which can become as damaging to Western economies as the withholding of oil.

3. Soviet and Chinese Policies

Unlike the Chinese People's Republic, the Soviet Union is a global power in fact and not merely by aspiration. There is no reason to suppose that the Soviet leadership has ever departed from the permanent aim of the Soviet State since its inception in 1917, which is to impose Soviet-style communism on the entire world. Since an aim as sweeping as this must seem Utopian, one can only note that is quite frequently reaffirmed, a striking expression of it being the following:

> Peaceful co-existence does not spell an end to the struggle between the two world social systems. The struggle will continue between the proletariat and the bourgeoisie, between world socialism and imperialism, up to the complete and final victory of communism on a world scale.
> (*Pravda*, 22 August 1973)

The oil-producing countries and those of the African littoral that are the particular concern of this report are not excluded from the global strategy of the USSR. It is, of course, legitimate to ask whether such apocalyptic ideological statements as the one just quoted can be seriously regarded as a guide to Soviet policies. The short answer is that they can, but only as a periodic reaffirmation of long-term aims that serves, *inter alia,* the purpose of justifying the ruling Communist Party's permanent monopoly of power. However, allowing for local setbacks and tactical reverses, the external evidences are entirely consistent with the politico-strategic aims re-expressed by *Pravda* August 1973, and with countless other Soviet statements, including speeches by the party leader, Brezhnev. On the basis of both ideological and practical evidence, it may be said that Soviet aims, both in the world as a whole and in the geographical regions under review, fall into two distinct categories:

1. *Long-term.* The fostering of Marxist governments subservient to Moscow.

2. *Medium-term.* The establishment of a system of client States, dependent upon Soviet supplies of arms and advisers.

In the Middle East the Russians are more visibly playing a super-Power game than in Africa (especially if, in an area in which geographical divisions do not correspond with religious or political affinities, Egypt is included in the "Middle East"). The fourth Arab-Israeli war of October 1973, and subsequent developments, demonstrated, more strikingly than before, the extent of Arab military dependence on the Soviet Union. Russia's ill-tempered but passive response to President Nixon's nuclear alert of 25 October showed, however, that fear of a direct confrontation with the United States and a desire to preserve the special relationship between the two super-Powers take precedence, in "the moment of truth", over the role of protecting power. Having said this, Soviet aims in the Middle East may be listed thus:

i. To step into the vacuum created by the departure of British power and establish hegemony over the entire area. Clearly, this is a long-term aim.
ii. In pursuance of this ultimate objective, to foster the emergence of client States (Iraq, Syria, Egypt); to frustrate Chinese penetration; to remove or reduce American influence (stopping short of confrontation).
iii. To gain control over some or all the major oil sources, both for Soviet and satellite needs and for the leverage to be gained over Western Europe, Japan and to a much lesser extent, the US, by making their imports of Middle East oil dependent upon Soviet goodwill. (Although the Soviet Union exports oil it does so partly at the expense of industry; moreover, the Warsaw Pact area needs at least 100 million tons a year in addition to the similar amount imported from Russia).
iv. To re-open the Suez Canal. This would enable Russia's powerful Mediterranean Fleet to join forces

with the necessarily much weaker Soviet naval presence in the Indian Ocean and enormously increase Russia's strategic ability to interfere with the Cape oil route. (It is not suggested that such interference is envisaged at this moment; but it cannot be excluded at a time of grave international crisis. An improvement in Russia's capacity to intervene is therefore not something to be dismissed as of little account.)

In Stalin's day, when permanent hostility to the non-Communist world prevailed, the visible countenance of Soviet foreign policy was monolithic. If there were any differences between party and government, they were not normally perceptible. Nowadays, contradictions are often in evidence. To some extent this is due to the greater sophistication of Soviet methods under Stalin's successors (and especially under Khrushchev's). It is also, however, due to the wide gap between Marxist-Leninist theory and the real world. Ideally, Soviet policy should be furthered by local Communist Parties obedient to Soviet directives. In reality, and especially in the two areas under discussion, there are very few orthodox Communist Parties worthy of the name, and most of these are weak and outlawed. In Egypt and other countries the Russians have had on occasion to sacrifice local Communists in the interests of better State-to-State relations.

This is only one of the difficulties the Russians face. Among others is the fundamental incompatibility between Islam and atheistic Marxism-Leninism, which applies throughout the oil-producing countries of the Middle East, and equally in the Moslem areas of Africa. A further difficulty, peculiar to Africa, is the remoteness of indigenous conditions from the social assumptions of Marxism-Leninism.

The late Professor I.I. Potekhin of the Africa Institute, Academy of Science of the USSR, expressed awareness of this gap in his study, *Africa Looks to the Future* (1960) but dismissed it in the name of dogma. He declared that Africa had "a vocation for socialism". He quoted a number of differing African definitions of socialism, by such leaders as

Presidents Senghor (Senegal), Nyerere (Tanzania), Nkrumah (Ghana) and Nasser (Egypt), and by the Senegalese intellectual, Jacques Janvier, who wanted Africans to take Yugoslavia as a model. Potekhin, however, dismissed all these definitions as irrelevant and declared that the only true socialism, in Africa as elsewhere, was the Marxist variety. Africa could not be an exception to Marxist-Leninist theory. A fundamental argument of Potekhin's was that the advent of independence did not complete the process of de-colonisation. The last vestiges of colonialism must be removed. This meant the establishment of "independent" economies, with Communist economic assistance.

Political Parties of Africa (Moscow, 1970), a symposium of contributions by various party ideologists, was essentially a far more sophisticated exercise, interpreting the actual history of political parties in African Marxist-Leninist terms. In Africa as elsewhere, it was argued, political parties represented social class interests. Much attention was devoted to "revolutionary-democratic parties", such as those then declared to be in power in Guinea, Republic of the Congo (Brazzaville), Tanzania, Algeria and Egypt. To these were added Ghana until the overthrow of Nkrumah in 1966, and Mali until 1968. It was argued, by implication, that such parties were necessary as part of the historical process in Africa, but that they would in time be superseded by true Communist parties. The section on the relatively few Communist parties in Africa declared that their common programme was "the creation of a State which will proceed along a road of non-capitalistic development — to socialism". There was a precise advocacy of a common anti-imperialist and democratic front with "revolutionary-democratic parties", to set African countries along the road to independence and progress.

One more document should be mentioned: the *World Communist Declaration* of 1960, which is relevant and important on two counts. One is that it was the last international Communist statement to be endorsed by both

Moscow and Peking. It committed China as well as Russia to the view that "peaceful co-existence" means the intensification of the international class struggle; that is, in plain language, of the fight unto death between communism and capitalism (meaning in practice all non-Communist systems, since communism, as defined in Moscow, is held to be bound to prevail everywhere in an unstated future).

The other important point about the 1960 Declaration is that it defined the concept of "independent States of national democracy", evidently to meet such cases as those of Cuba, Guinea and Mali. To qualify for this title a State would have to fight "imperialism" (that is, the Western countries), oppose (Western) military bases on its soil, give full democratic rights to "the people" (that is, the local Communist Party, or in default of one, "revolutionary-democratic" parties — a later refinement), and show its readiness to introduce "democratic" (that is, socialist) reforms that would pave the way for communism. In reality, communism, whether of the Moscow or the Peking variety, still appears to be a rather distant prospect, in Africa as in the Middle East. In the medium term, however, the Russians have pursued with single-minded application the aim of setting up client States wherever the opportunity arose. It must be added that in this attempt, they have suffered a number of reverses, e.g.:

Egypt. A client State, amounting at one time to a satellite, had in fact been fostered successfully, but the satellisation process ended abruptly with the expulsion of some 20,000 Russian military and civilian advisers by President Sadat on 18 July 1972. The renewed Arab-Israeli war late last year, however, enabled the Russians to re-establish themselves as the indispensable providers of military aid for the Arabs, in Syria as well as in Egypt.

Sudan. The Moscow-line Communist Party briefly seized power in July 1971, and the coup leaders immediately made contact with the Soviet Ambassador. This success lasted only three days, and the President, General Nimeiry, regained control. As a result, the party was decimated.

Zaire (ex-Belgian Congo). Twice in a little over three years

— in September 1960 and in November 1963 — the entire staff of the Soviet embassy in Leopoldville (now Kinshasa) were expelled, in each case after the introduction of Soviet arms and agents.

Ghana. When President Nkrumah fell in February 1966, 1,100 Russians left or were expelled. It was later disclosed that they had been involved in supporting the Nkrumah regime in extensive subversive activities in other African countries.

Republic of Guinea. In December 1961, the Soviet Ambassador, Daniel Solod, was expelled from Conakry. The left-wing government later blamed him for having been behind serious disturbances the previous month.

Especially since the collapse of the Soviet subversive campaign conducted from Ghana, the Russians have been more selective and cautious in their clandestine activity in Africa. They have tended on the whole to cultivate good State-to-State relations with African governments and in two major countries (Nigeria and the Sudan) they assisted the government against local rebellions: that is, against the separatist army in Biafra, and against the Anya-Nya rebels in the southern Sudan. They continue, however, to provide extensive training facilities, arms and some money, for African terrorists and guerillas, but in a more discriminating way than formerly.

The beneficiaries of their semi-clandestine aid are groups or movements that most closely conform to the "revolutionary-democratic" label and are most likely, if ever they are successful, to set up revolutionary governments susceptible to Soviet influence. These include FRELIMO (Mozambique), MPLA (Angola), ZAPU (Rhodesia), ANC (South Africa), SWAPO (South-West Africa), and PAIGC (Portuguese Guinea). Some aid is provided in monetary form through the Organisation for African Unity (OAU). But greater store is set by the training and indoctrination of individuals in the Soviet Union, either at special camps for non-Communist revolutionaries in Moscow, Tashkent and Odessa, or in the specialised facilities of the Lenin Institute (reserved for Moscow-line

Communists from the non-Communist world) in Moscow. During 1973, a development worth noting in this context was the technological escalation in Portuguese Guinea (Guinea-Bissau), where the PAIGC guerillas are now equipped with portable Soviet-made SA-7 missiles. One of these, indeed, was used to shoot down a jet aircraft carrying the Portuguese air force commander in Guinea, Almeida Brito, who was killed.

Soviet aid to the PAIGC must be seen in the context of Moscow's interest in that organisation's territorial base in the neighbouring Republic of Guinea, whose capital, Conakry, provides the Russians with useful naval port facilities. Guinea is one of the very few African countries professing to practise "scientific socialism", but in fact the participatory "democracy" in that country is much closer to the Chinese than to the Soviet model. This is one reason why the Russians are cautious there; others are the expulsion of their ambassador some years ago (see above) and the fact that the country's weak economy is heavily dependent on foreign private extracting companies.

At the moment, the nearest thing to a Soviet client State in Africa is the strategically situated Somali Republic, in the Horn of Africa. One of the poorest of African countries, Somali, like Guinea, has opted for "scientific socialism" under the military regime of General Siad Barre. This claim is not necessarily accepted in Moscow which, however, makes encouraging sounds from time to time. General Siad faces the problem of explaining to his almost exclusively Moslem people that scientific socialism need not clash with Islam. That is one difficulty; another is that the regime lacks a political party or organisation. The defect is to be remedied by a course of ideological indoctrination now being conducted in orientation centres scattered through the country.

Meanwhile, the Russians have trained the Somali army of 15,000, equipped it with 150 tanks and more than 300 armoured personnel carriers; the air force has Soviet MiG-15 and 17 fighters. More directly relevant to this report is the fact that the Russians have built a deep water port at

Berbera. There, and at Kismayu and Mogadishu, the Russians have extensive facilities for their expanding Indian Ocean fleet. Shrewdly, the Somalis have not allowed their dependence on the Russians to spoil relations with China, and the Chinese economic aid outstrips the Russian. On the whole, however, the Chinese influence remains slight in Somalia.

The Sudan in the east and Nigeria in the west are other arenas of Sino-Soviet rivalry in littoral States. The Russians gained some advantage over the Chinese by providing the Federal Government of Nigeria with military equipment during the Biafran war. But the Nigerians paid for all they received, thus retaining their political independence. In the field of agitation and propaganda, the Russians have been handicapped since 1966 by the ban on political parties, including the (Communist) Socialist Workers' and Farmers' Party. They continue, however, to train party officials in the USSR and pay them salaries. In the Sudan, the collapse of the Communist coup in 1971 gave the Chinese the chance to move in with military aid, first announced in April 1972 and consisting of a brigade of tanks and eight MiG 17 planes.

The map appearing with this section gives the latest available figures of Soviet representatives in the oil-producing countries of the Middle East and in Africa. In each case, the number of suspected or positively identified members of the intelligence services is also given. The majority of those belong to the main Soviet secret police and espionage organisation, the KGB (Committee of State Security); the others, to the military espionage organisation, the GRU (Chief Intelligence Directorate, attached to the Soviet general staff). It will be seen that in these areas as in all others, the opening of diplomatic relations with the Soviet Union entails a KGB presence as well. (The negative advantage of not having diplomatic relations — as with Saudi Arabia and certain other Gulf States — is that they are spared the KGB presence. It does not follow that they are entirely free of Soviet agents; but these are denied the close supervision and other facilities available to KGB officers under diplomatic cover.)

As is true elsewhere, the activities of KGB or GRU officers tend to be tolerated by the host countries until they become flagrant, when expulsions may result. In recent years there has been nothing comparable in scale to the Soviet network in Ghana, mentioned earlier; and expulsions or departures after discovery have been on a relatively small scale. Here are some recent examples:

Ghana. On 21 January 1974, the First Secretary and consular officer of the Soviet embassy in Accra, Valentin Fomenko, was arrested for alleged espionage. He was sent home within 72 hours. Fomenko was said to have been arrested near the racecourse when receiving "very secret papers" from an army officer. Reporting these events, the Accra weekly *Palaver* recalled two earlier expulsions of Soviet "diplomats": Valter Vinogradov for subversive activities (May 1971); and Guennad Petrovich Potemkin, commercial officer of the Soviet trade delegation, for espionage (July 1971).

In an editorial, the paper said that Ghana, striving to restore its ruined economy, "cannot afford to allow its national security to be toyed with by countries which pretend to be friends of developing countries while subverting them under the cover of diplomacy". *(Palaver,* 23 January). Another comment was: "The USSR profess to help us, then why not help us? Spying on us is not helping us". *(The Echo,* an independent Accra weekly, 27 January).

Senegal. In mid-1973, a KGB officer, Oleg Bezrodny, was withdrawn from the country by the Soviet authorities after complaints from the Senegalese government, which also refused to renew the visa of Georgi Shevchenko.

Mali. In April 1972, the government expelled three Soviet officials: Lev Yatsin, Ivan Lyssykh and Vitali Potchankin.

It is worth noting that KGB men expelled from one country quite often turn up in another, sometimes without even a change of identity. Thus three KGB men expelled from Kenya in March 1966 are, or have been, in similar posts elsewhere since their expulsion. They are: Yuri V. Kuritsin, who was the correspondent of the Soviet features agency

Novosti. He is now in Nigeria under the same cover; Yuri Yukalov, who was a First Secretary at the Soviet embassy in Nairobi. He is now in Dar-es-Salaam (Tanzania); Vladimir Godakov, who was also a First Secretary in Nairobi. He was last *en poste* as Counsellor in Tripoli (Libya).

In general, the Chinese approach to Africa has been markedly less ideological than the Soviet. At one time they were apparently prepared to support almost any group, whatever the persuasion, that was in arms. In 1964, Chou En-lai startled African politicians by declaring that "revolutionary prospects are excellent throughout Africa". Later, the Chinese diplomatic missions were expelled from Burundi, and from Niger, Dahomey and the Central African Republic, where they were blamed from plots against the regimes in those countries. They, too, learned from these setbacks. Since then, they have concentrated on outstripping the Russians in economic aid and attempting to do the same in aid to revolutionary movements. Some of their activities have been noted.

By far the largest Chinese aid project has been the construction of the Tanzam railway, which has given Peking considerable influence over, and a disguised military presence in, Tanzania. Chinese guerrilla instructors have been serving in training camps in that country. Both there and in China they have trained guerrillas and terrorists in various movements, including ZANU (Rhodesia) and FRELIMO (Mozambique) as well as various splinter groups from the latter. On the western side of the continent they have been making strong efforts to woo the MPLA (Angola) away from its predominant Soviet influence, so far without decisive success.

Sino-Soviet rivalry and competitive subversion must be seen realistically. Since both countries work against Western interests their rivalry does not benefit the West, and complicates life for local security organisations and foreign intelligence services. On the other hand, China's effort undoubtedly constitutes a further barrier to Soviet expansion in the area, which otherwise, would be hindered only by local resistance to Soviet pressures and blandishments; since Africa, unlike the Middle East, is an area of minimum American involvement where a Soviet-American confrontation is less likely than elsewhere.

The size of the Chinese effort in the areas of interest to this report naturally prompts questions. For the past two or three years Chinese economic aid in Africa has greatly exceeded Soviet, both in absolute terms and as a proportion of total assistance by each country. Moreover, Peking's aid to revolutionary movements in Africa and the Arab world (most notably to the PFLOAG (Popular Front for the Liberation of Oman and the Arab Gulf) rebels in the Dhofar area of Oman) though impossible to estimate with any accuracy, probably exceeds its aid to similar organisations on China's doorstep in South-East Asia. It seems reasonable to suppose that this difference is in part accounted for by the fact that in Africa at least, for China as well as Russia, a confrontation with America is not a visible danger, whereas in South-East Asia it has been and probably still is.

There remain unanswered questions about the return which the Chinese must expect for their large overt and clandestine investment in countries along the Cape oil route. In the Middle East, especially, it must be surmised that the Chinese have an ultimate interest — as the Russians have — in gaining some control over sources of oil.

In Africa, China's interest could well be demographic. With the exceptions of Thailand, Burma and possibly Cambodia the countries of South-East Asia tend to be overcrowded and are mostly net importers of rice. Africa offers relatively underpopulated areas with an economic potential which the Chinese may believe they are better qualified to exploit than more advanced countries. Such motives, if they exist, are left unstated. A broader political ambition that can more readily be inferred from Chinese statements is that of becoming the leader of the Third World, or as they prefer to put it, of the "intermediate zones" opposed to both the super-Powers.

One thing is certain. Any victories for revolutionary movements in southern Africa would produce regimes indebted either to the Soviet Union or to China, or both. Any such outcome to Africa's guerrilla wars, or to the struggle for power in various countries, would threaten all Western interests, and not least the security of the Cape oil route.

4. Revolutionary and political challenges in the Gulf

For the purposes of this study it is assumed that: (a) some *modus vivendi* will be found for the Arab-Israeli crisis that will induce Saudi Arabia and the other producer States which follow her lead to cease to use the withdrawal of oil as a political weapon; and (b) in addition, means will be found to encourage them to increase production towards the level required by the expansion of Western economies. We now have to consider whether there may be revolutionary and political challenges in the Gulf area to the continuing flow of oil by the Cape Route. Revolutionary movements are active, to greater or less degree, in all the Persian Gulf countries, but, in the main, they are being contained, and we shall discuss them as potential rather than actual dangers.

There is, however, one potential threat which transcends frontiers. Two days after the Arab-Israeli war began the *rapporteur* of this Study Group discussed the situation with Yusif Sayegh, president of the Palestinian Liberation Fund, in Beirut. Sayegh is a professor at the American University of Beirut, an impressive, highly articulate man. He gave as his personal view that the Palestine Liberation Organisation could not tolerate any solution of the Middle East conflict which left Israel as a sovereign State. The Palestinians, however, had no quarrel with the Israeli people and were prepared to live amicably side by side with them within the boundaries of an Arab State, and would not discriminate against them in trade or any other way.

On the other hand, he said, if the Arab countries accepted a solution based on the 1967 United Nations Resolution the PLO, well armed and well supplied with funds, would fight for their rights, attacking each Arab government through its own people until their demands were met or the government collapsed. It is true that Sayegh's remarks were made in an atmosphere of of euphoria, at a time when Israel appeared to be losing the war, and he may have been afraid that Egypt and Syria would behave too leniently to a conquered nation. Certainly, in recent PLO statements some willingness for compromise has been shown, but it would seem very likely that, whatever solution for the Arab-Israeli conflict is found, the more extreme sections of the PLO will not accept it, and may indeed turn against the Arab countries that have subsidized them for so long.

According to *The Times* of 3 January, 1974, "Apart from helping the IRA Colonel Khadaffi's regime has allocated £45 million to Black September, the clandestine wing of Fatah, and £20 million to other *fedayeen* groups". The newspaper added that there is a branch of Black September, known as the National Youth for the Liberation of Palestine, which is wholly financed by the Libyans. With this kind of backing, and bearing in mind Khadaffi's attitude to the Gulf States, the possibility of sabotage operations by the Palestinian extremists against oil installations and tanker traffic in the Gulf cannot be discounted.

One of the unpleasant facts of life today is that money — and plenty of money — appears to be distributed with the utmost irresponsibility to almost any movement that seeks to strike a blow against society. Once the money is given, the movement has to strike, if only to ensure that the supply continues. Terrorism has become for many young people an attractive, adventurous way of life, and the new weapons, such as the SA-7 heat-homing missiles and remote-controlled bombs and mines, reduce the danger of detection and arrest to a minimum. Thus subversive factions in a country can often get without difficulty all the money, weapons and trained operatives they require to enforce their arguments. If, therefore, this Report appears to see subversive elements behind every desert palm, they are not necessarily figments of imagination, but real men and women out to cause trouble.

There are two reasons why smaller States in the Gulf are

vulnerable to subversion. One is that in most cases government rests on a shifting layer of expatriates — Palestinian civil servants, Jordanian, Pakistani and Western soldiers, exiled Iraqi advisers and Egyptian teachers. In many of the States these essential members of the infrastructure are still treated as foreigners and not allowed rights of citizenship. Except among the ruling families there is no tradition of public service. The framework of government in many cases is held together by personal loyalty or enforced subservience to the Ruler. This is fertile ground for corruption and subversion, and the continuance of any of the smaller States in the present form is problematical.

The other reason is simply a question of wealth. In Mr. Akins' paper "The Oil Crisis: The Wolf is Here" (*Foreign Affairs*, April 1973) he estimated that Abu Dhabi might be receiving oil revenues of $1,500 million in 1975, and $5,000 million in 1980. (These figures are likely to be greatly exceeded.) It is obvious that for a country of 100,000 people, with little chance of economic development, the financial structure is grossly top-heavy, and must be a standing temptation to the have-nots in neighbouring territories. The fact that Abu Dhabi is wisely governed, and that everything possible is being done within its borders, including a subsidy of about £800 a year for every head of family, plus a free house, electricity, water and telephone, and all expenses connected with schooling, does not necessarily make for a stable society.

Historically, great accessions of unearned wealth have resulted in trouble for the States that received them. Equally the dangers that can arise from too much money and too many idle hands are present in the Gulf States. Some of their rich young men, who have attended European universities, come to regard their own paternalistic societies as outmoded and ripe for a change. It may be expected that Iran, with by far the best and best-equipped armed forces in the area and a vital interest in preserving the status quo, will not tolerate serious trouble inside the Gulf area, and this question is considered later.

5. Security in the Producing Countries

We will deal first with Oman and then with the principal oil States, proceeding from the Straits of Hormuz to the head of the Gulf.

Oman

This is an independent Sultanate in special relationship with the UK. It has a population of about 75,000, an army of 5,500 men, a navy of 200 and an air force of 300. Sultan Sayed Qabus bin Said deposed his father in 1970 and has since led the country in a dramatic leap forward towards a more modern society. His task is formidable, since 95 per cent of Omanis are illiterate, and although there are now sixty schools instead of three in Sultan Said's time, good teachers are lacking and it will take a generation before the employment of expatriates in every branch of administration can be dispensed with.

There has been a revolutionary challenge in Oman since 1963, formed by the Popular Front for the Liberation of Oman and the Arab Gulf (PFLOAG) which is based in South Yemen (PDRY) and has been given much help by the Chinese and the Soviets. PFLOAG, originally a nationalist movement, later became dominated by Marxist ideas and in December 1971 expressed its support for the "Palestine revolution" and declared its opposition to Zionism and its intention to wage a people's war throughout South-Eastern Arabia. Large areas of Dhofar were occupied and there was some acceptance, particularly by the animist tribes in the mountainous interior, of Marxist-Leninist teaching. This was a Maoist-type attempt to stir up a peasant revolution.

A determined action, Operation Jaguar, by the Sultan's armed forces defeated the insurgents and liberated most of the fertile area around Salalah and Mirbat. Units of the British SAS Regiment were used in this campaign and there was also support from Jordanian and Iranian troops. The Oman forces are officered mainly by expatriates — British and some Jordanian seconded or contract officers in the higher ranks, with the help of Iranian training units. In the opinion of a senior British military adviser the insurgents have been contained, at least temporarily, and although the war can never end neatly, it can be reduced to an acceptable level in about three years. Omani NCOs and junior officers are being trained intensively, and it will soon be possible to put an Omani-commanded rifle company into the field.

In recent months the Chinese presence has been less obvious and fewer Chinese arms have been captured. The Chinese advisers and trainers appear to have withdrawn to Aden. Over 700 insurgents have fled to the Sultan's forces, including three political commissars and six officers of the Ho Chi Minh and Lenin units of the PFLOAG guerrillas. But PFLOAG is still very much alive. There have been no instances of sophisticated sabotage, apart from two attempts to sink tankers, which are mentioned below. But PFLOAG propaganda is widespread, and has an important outlet through the South Yemen Embassy in Beirut. It is known that the movement has succeeded in infiltrating the security forces in the Arab Emirates and it cannot be assumed that because its "people's war" has not gained ground, its capacity for subversion is any less.

The Omanis are tough, likeable and independent, and learn quickly when given the chance. They have a long tradition as a sea-faring nation, and are proud of their position in sharing, with Iran, the control of the gateway to the Gulf. Iran is, in fact, concerned to ensure that Oman continues to resist subversion, and the provision of funds and training cadres is said to be increasing. The United Arab Emirates also regard Oman as their protection against the focus of Marxist infection in Aden, and Abu Dhabi has helped to provice funds for the war. Saudi Arabia has given, it appears, even more and is prepared to send in troops if necessary.

To sum up, there seems every hope that the ambitions of PFLOAG to win a people's war in Oman will be frustrated by the Sultan's armed forces, with some help from their friends. But PFLOAG has a secure base in the PDRY, and will try other means of achieving its ends. Sheikh Omar, Director General of Information in Muscat — and like many of the senior executives of the Sultan's Government, a Zanzibar Omani — sees the long-term danger in the young people who, as they return from foreign universities, bring back revolutionary ideas. There is already a good deal of unrest among the educated youth of Muscat and its twin city, Matrah, and some of this is attributed to the men who, in the time of Sultain Said, were obliged to go abroad illegally to get their education and attended universities in Communist bloc countries.

PFLOAG has already attempted to attack oil targets in Oman, and special precautions have been taken by Petroleum Development (Oman), a company owned as to 85 per cent by Shell, and 15 per cent by the Campagnie Française des Pétroles and by Gulbenkian interests. There was an abortive attempt in 1970 to seize a fort which commands the Sumail gap in northern Oman, through which the long pipeline from the Fahud field to the shore terminal at Mina al Fahal, west of Muscat, runs. Two attempts were made, one with limpet mines, to sabotage tankers at the terminal, but both were discovered in time. Although fishing in the bay has been banned it is impossible to stop fishing boats from passing through it, especially at night. A new berth is being constructed to accommodate 500,000 tankers, and they will be given special protection.

It should, perhaps, be added that an attempt was made by the Chinese-trained PFLOAG guerrillas in 1971 to occupy the Omani enclave at the tip of the Ras Musandam peninsula, at the entrance to the Straits of Hormuz. This may have been a diversionary operation to draw off the Sultan's troops who were threatening the guerrillas in the south. Whatever the purpose, the attempt failed. The risk that the southern side of the Straits might fall into Communist hands is not now taken very seriously, because it seems certain that Iran would not allow this to happen, and there is apparently an ancient Persian claim to the Cape which might be invoked as an excuse.

The Straits of Hormuz

The Straits are, of course, the most vulnerable point along the whole route. Close the 50-mile gap, and you halt the flow of oil immediately. But no naval power could turn the tankers back to their loading ports except in a state of war or in an international situation of such gravity that the risk of at least local war could be accepted. There remains the possibility of peacetime action, either ascribable to a revolutionary movement like PFLOAG, or "unattributably", perhaps by the use of a submarine. Traffic through the Straits is so dense that there would be a good chance of sinking or crippling one ship. And one would be quite enough for propaganda effect.

This is the kind of reprisal action that the Palestinian extremists might conceivably use, because it would hit at producer and consumer States indiscriminately. A nuclear submarine could, of course, pick its target and attack without betraying its presence.

On the other hand, it is very largely against the risk of interference with the oil route that the Iranian navy and the new naval base at Bandar Abbas have been built up so rapidly, and the reaction would be immediate. Within a very short time, perhaps even before British, United States or Soviet ships could be called on to help, there would be convoys of tankers through the Straits with Iranian naval protection, and even the Abu Dhabi navy might contribute the six 25-knot Vosper Thorneycroft patrol boats which they ordered recently.

Thus the effect of, say, a mining operation, unless it could be repeated without detection, would be only temporary, if damaging. To a revolutionary movement the propaganda value, however, would be considerable. For the VLCCs there is no way, under normal conditions, of catching sight of a floating mine in time, since there is as a rule no bow look-out. It is on the bridge, hundreds of feet astern, that the watches are kept, and from there it is impossible to see any small floating object in the sea nearer than about a mile and a half owing to the line of sight. (Tanker crews admit that they can run down a fishing boat and not know until the bows of their ships are examined in port.)

In times of crisis big tankers have kept special watches, but this means ten extra men — one in command and three watches of three — and the expense and inconvenience is such that the procedure is kept up for as short a time as possible. Unless, therefore, there has been a clear warning to keep a special watch for trouble at sea a floating mine, or a small vessel strewing mines directly in the path of a VLCC would, in all probability, escape notice, particularly at night, and if damage resulted it would be impossible to attribute the blame unless the perpetrator chose to claim responsibility.

It was to ensure the free passage of oil carriers through the Straits that the Shah claimed the islands of Abu Musa and the two Tumbs, lying just inside the Gulf, when the British withdrew from the area in 1971. He landed troops on the three islands a day before British protection ended, on 30 November. There were counter claims, but by and large the *fait accompli* has been accepted — with some sweetening of the Sheikh of Sharjah from the Iranian treasury. Nevertheless, it is interesting to note that Colonel Khadaffi actually threatened to send Arab guerrillas to take back the islands. He did not do so, but took his revenge on the British, who had not opposed the Shah's action, by nationalising BP assets in Libya. Yet the fact that he could even conceive of such action, over 2,000 miles away from Libya, poses the possibility that if interference with traffic through the Straits should occur it would not necessarily be by movements or powers in the vicinity.

The Union of Arab Emirates

When the British began to withdraw their support from the Gulf in 1968 it was hoped to form a Federation of all the British-protected States — Bahrein, Qatar, Abu Dhabi, Dubai, Sharjah, Umm al Qwain, Ajman, Ras al Kaimah and Fujaira — but in the end the largest States, Bahrein and Qatar, achieved separate independence. Of the seven which form the UAE, Abu Dhabi and Dubai, being the most important, provide between them the President, Vice-President, and the President of the Federal Council of Ministers.

Abu Dhabi is immensely rich in oil reserves, Dubai moderately so, and Sharjah has only small reserves. The other four States have none. This situation has caused much unrest among the poorer members, and in 1972 Egypt attempted to exploit the situation in an attempt to set up its own nominee as Ruler of Sharjah. The deposed Sheikh, Saqr bin Sultan, who had been in exile in Egypt, tried to oust the ruling Sheikh, his cousin Khalid bin Mohammed, with the help of a small band of followers armed with Russian hand grenades and Kalashnikov automatic rifles. The coup failed owing to the prompt action of the British-officered Union Defence Force, but the seeds of revolt remain, in spite of hand-outs from the richer States.

The main hope that PFLOAG may have of achieving one of its declared ends, and bringing a form of Communism to the UAE, probably lies in sponsoring similar forms of rebellion. To prevent this Abu Dhabi and Dubai have built up strong security and offensive forces and still retain British officers in command, and other ranks. As time goes on the gradual replacement of these officers and the lack of co-operation between the two police forces and between the Union Defence Force (formerly the Trucial Oman Scouts) and the Abu Dhabi Defence Force (recruited and paid directly by the Ruler) could form a fertile ground for revolt. A senior oil executive in Abu Dhabi said recently: "There is no answer to the security problem."

Abu Dhabi has a fast-growing population of about 100,000 people, a large, ill-defined patch of desert, no water and a great deal of oil in the ground. Size for size, it is the richest country in the world. Until the present crisis the on-shore wells, in the hands of the Abu-Dhabi Petroleum Company (BP, Shell, the Compagnie Française des Pétroles, Exxon, Mobil and Partex) were producing at the rate of 1.3 mbd and it was expected that the offshore installations of the Abu Dhabi Marine Areas (BP, CFP and a Japanese interest) would be producing, by 1975, 1.75 mbd.

The principal fields are at Bab and Bu Hasa, in the desert south-west of Abu Dhabi city, and at Um Shaif (offshore). The existing production is from Bab and Bu Hasa and the crude is de-gassed at Habshan and then pumped through a 90-mile, 24-inch pipe to the Jebel Dhanna Terminal on the coast. There is also a gas pipeline to Abu Dhabi city. The oil terminal has tanks of 400,000 ton capacity on rising ground from which it flows by gravity through under-water pipes to three sea-loading berths capable of accommodating VLCCs for partial loading and tankers up to 90,000 tons deadweight for complete loading. The hinterland to these installations is desert stretching back to the Omani frontier. They are singularly vulnerable to attack by a determined group of guerrillas, if so inclined.

There is more oil underground in the rich Zarrara fields in the south and on the Omani border near Al Ain oasis, better known to us, perhaps, by the name of Buraimi, one of its villages. Until a few years ago the oasis was used as a watering place by tribes from the whole area, and no one bothered about its ownership. When Britain drew the frontiers it gave six of the villages to Abu Dhabi and three to Oman, in spite of the fact that the whole area, as well as Zarrara, is claimed by Saudi Arabia. The discovery of oil exacerabated the situation, but recently Saudi Arabia and Abu Dhabi have agreed to hold a plebiscite to determine where local loyalties lie. The Zarrara fields are still disputed, and therefore undeveloped.

In general, although relations between Abu Dhabi and Saudi Arabia are still strained, they have improved, and there is now a Saudi agent in Abu Dhabi, although still no exchange of diplomatic missions. The Ruler, Sheikh Zaid, did not, until the recent war, hold strong opinions about the Israeli problem, but he followed King Faisal in oil questions, at least up to a point. It is still unclear whether he ever acted on the decision to cut back 25 per cent in November. Hitherto, he has spent his oil revenues (likely to total several thousand million dollars in 1974) on internal

Indian Ocean Leaders 1974

Above Left: B. J. Vorster, Prime Minister of South Africa

Above: E. G. Whitlam, Prime Minister of Australia

Centre: Julius Nyerere, President of Tanzania

Below Left: Mrs Indira Gandhi, Prime Minister of India

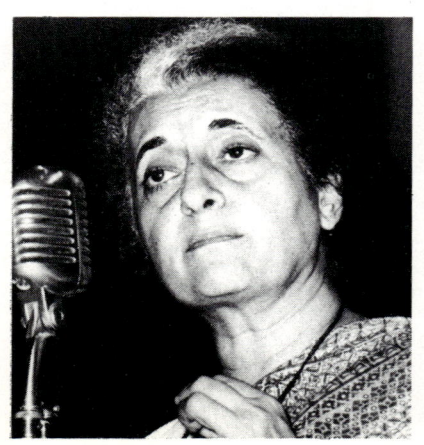

Below: Ahmad Hassan al Bakr, President of Iraq

Soviet *Kashin* class destroyer, 4,300 tons, on passage to the Indian Ocean rounding the Cape of Good Hope

Soviet fleet support ship accompanying the helicopter cruiser *Leningrad* and destroyer

Soviet helicopter cruiser *Leningrad*, 17,000 tons, on passage round the Cape to the Indian Ocean

A Russian naval squadron passed the Cape early in July 1974 on its way to the Indian Ocean from the Atlantic. The *Leningrad* carries 18 helicopters for anti-submarine work, surface-to-air missiles, an anti-submarine launcher, 57 mm guns and two quintuple torpedo tubes. The *Kashin* class destroyer is equipped with surface-to-air missiles, 3 inch guns and five torpedo tubes. The squadron appeared in October 1974, rounded the Cape en route for Fernando Po, and was expected to proceed to Dakar, Senegal, before returning to base in the Black Sea

Soviet *Amur* class repair ship PM-129, 140 miles south of Knysna, South Africa, on 20th February, 1974. One of these ships is usually in Basra or Umm Qasr, presumably supporting the Iraqi navy

This Soviet oceanographic research ship *Bashkiriya* of the *Akademik Kurchatov* class displaces 6,700 tons. She was sighted 140 miles south of Knysna on 20th February 1974 en route to the Indian Ocean. This is one of a class of four, a very modern type of research vessel, which has been used in all the world's oceans, and indicates the USSR's great interest in oceanographic research

The *Kresta II* class guided missile cruiser, *Marshal Vorishilov*, heading north-east with a Soviet naval squadron, 140 miles south of Knysna. She is the fifth of seven ships of the class and displays comprehensive electronic fittings, surface-to-air and surface-to-surface missiles, torpedo tubes and twin 76 mm guns. She will spend some time operating in the Indian Ocean before joining the Soviet Pacific fleet

Indian Ocean Leaders 1974

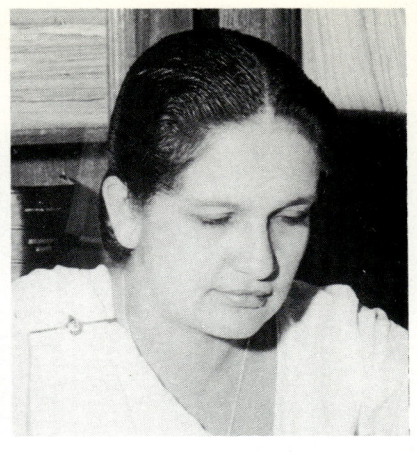

Above Left: Sheikh Mujibur Rahman, Prime Minister of Bangladesh

Above: Mrs S. D. Bandaranaike, Prime Minister of Sri Lanka

Centre: Z. A. Bhutto, Prime Minister of Pakistan

Below Left: Sir Seewoosagur Ramgoolam, Prime Minister of Mauritius

Below: Lee Kuan Yew, Prime Minister of Singapore

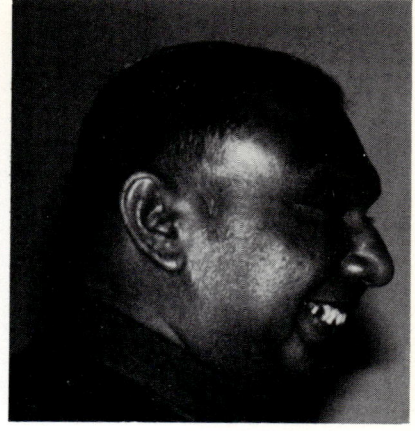

Indian Ocean Leaders 1974

Above Left: General Jaafar al Nimeiri, President of Sudan

Above: Ahmed Zaki, Prime Minister of Maldive Islands

Centre: General Siad Barre, President of Somalia

Below Left: Jomo Kenyatta, President of Kenya

Below: Joaqim Chissano, FRELIMO'S frontrunner in Mozambique

Indian Ocean Leaders 1974

Above Left: The Shah of Iran

Above: Anwar al Sadat, President of Egypt

Centre: Salem Roubia Ali, President of the People's Democratic Republic of Yemen (Aden)

Below Left: King Faisal of Saudi Arabia

Below: Sultan Qaboos of Oman

development, and indeed the island on which the capital is built has been given fine roads and buildings, and a great effort is being made to create jobs. There are good schools and hospitals and, as noted elsewhere in this Report, every native head of family is very well provided for. Foreigners, who make up a quarter of the population, are not so lucky. According to David Housego (*Financial Times*, 3 January 1974) Omanis, Bahrainis and Qataris, can obtain citizenship after three years, other Arab expatriates after working five years before and five years after 1972, and non-Arabs only after ten years before 1972 and 20 years afterwards.

It is estimated, Mr. Housego reported, that Sheikh Zaid gave $500 million to the "front-line" Arab States in recent months and proposes to provide them further with no less than $1,000 million. In September he contracted to borrow $200 million from Morgan Grenfell, of which $180 million was spent in buying Soviet arms for Syria and Egypt. Thus it is clear that for the time being Abu Dhabi can find uses for its total income from oil revenues. But it was decided in the spring of 1973 that the State's income was increasing at such an astronomical rate that further exploration for oil must be curbed.

The whole system of government in Abu Dhabi is one of benevolent paternalism, and the Sheikh is accustomed to dealing with his subjects' complaints personally, and with absolute authority. He is regarded as a wise and dedicated ruler, who commands the respect of the expatriates who administer government under him. Nevertheless, the task of converting the whole of his country into a modern State is a daunting one, and as the population grows so will the number of feather-bedded Abu Dhabians.

Dubai has about 80,000 inhabitants, of whom 95 per cent live in the city. Its hinterland, like Abu Dhabi's, has little value for either agricultural or industrial exploitation, but it does provide sweet water, whereas almost all the supplies of Abu Dhabi city come from the distillation of sea water. The great difference between the two cities is that whereas Abu Dhabi, until the accession of Sheikh Zaid, was a backward, overgrown village, Dubai has steadily developed throughout this century as the main trading port in the southern Gulf. It has a broad creek that forms a natural harbour for general cargo vessels, and acts as entrepot for the surrounding states. Port Rashid, with impressive modern installations, was completed in 1972. Much of Dubai's prosperity, up to the discovery of oil, came from the fact that it allows free import and export of gold. The Ruler, Sheikh Rashid bin Sa'id al Maktoum is an enlightened and progressive prince who administers his State largely through expatriates, but with a growing admixture of local talent.

The two main offshore oilfields were discovered in 1966 and 1970 and given the name of Fateh. They produce about 300,000 bd at present, but exploration is continuing. The main concession is held by the Continental Oil Company (CONOCO). The Fateh fields are 58 miles from the shore, and it was therefore desirable to store, process and deliver the oil at sea. This is done by the use of well-platforms, a six-pile control production platform with separator facilities, two floating storage vessels with combined 600,000 barrel capacity, and two SPMs (single point moorings) for loading tankers. In addition, there is the main storage facility, composed of three 600,000 ton Khazzans. These are remarkable constructions, shaped like an inverted champagne glass, with a base diameter of 270 ft, topped by a tower that appears above the water. The Khazzans are pinned to the sea bed but are open at the bottom, so that water can flow in freely.

When oil is pumped in it remains on top of the sea water and pressure is maintained by the upthrust of the water beneath. Forty feet above sea-level a production and processing platform connects the towers of the three submerged Khazzans, and pipelines conduct the crude to the mooring buoys. There is no pipeline to the shore. Thus, the production of the Dubai Petroleum Company is not vulnerable to land attack. Any attempt to sabotage the offshore installations would require very sophisticated techniques and the use of considerable force.

Sheikh Rashid has found other means of absorbing his

surplus wealth besides Port Rashid. There is a new international airport which acts as a refuelling station for the Europe-Far East traffic, and work has already begun on the construction of a major ship repair facility, at an estimated cost of of $162 million. Taylor Woodrow and Costain Civil Engineering are undertaking the work, which it is hoped to complete by 1976. The new port will include, as well as conventional berths, three dry docks capable of servicing and repairing VLCCs: two for tankers up to 500,000 tons and one for one million-tonners.

The decision to construct the tanker facility at Dubai was made by the Sheikh in spite of the fact that the Organisation of Arab Petroleum Exporting Countries (OAPEC) had chosen Bahrein as the most appropriate site. It was based on the argument contained in a feasibility report prepared by John McMullen Associates Inc. of New York in which it was pointed out that the number of tankers loading in the Gulf in 1975 could be estimated at 800, of which 400 would be VLCCs, and that since VLCCs require dry-docking for maintenance and repair every 18 months there would, in effect, be ample business for everyone.

The report added that by 1980 the number of VLCCs would double, and that a large number of major oil companies and VLCC owners had confirmed that the siting of dry docks in the Gulf would be more attractive than the existing facilities available in Europe and the Far East. (There was no mention, in McMullen's news release, of Southern Africa where, as we shall see, both the South Africans and the Portuguese are going ahead with similar projects.) Although Dubai will have to compete in the Gulf with Bahrein there does appear to be a good argument for the new port provided, of course, that the growth rate of the oil flow increases sufficiently. From 1975 onwards, therefore, it is conceivable that sabotage attacks could be made on tankers undergoing repair at Dubai, but here again the operation would require great skill and heavy armed support.

Bahrein consists of one main island and thirty-two smaller ones, lying off the Saudi Arabian coast and the peninsula of Qatar. It has about 200,000 inhabitants. The Emir, Sheikh Isa bin Sulman al-Khalifa, allowed free elections in December 1972 and the elected Council of Ministers has formed a new constitution which includes an elected National Assembly.

The Bahreinis no longer produce much oil but aim to be the service centre for the Gulf. They have a large refinery, processing mainly Saudi Arabian crude, and their economy, helped by the ALBA aluminium smelter, which uses natural gas, is viable. There is little unemployment and labour for the construction of the dry dock projected by the OAPEC will have to be imported. There is some fear in the lower Gulf States that Bahrein is a hotbed of Communist intrigue. This is probably much exaggerated. It is true that PFLOAG elements are active in the island, and that many Bahreinis have been educated in Soviet bloc universities, but if there is subversion, it appears to be well contained, and the very fact that the members of the new Assembly will be elected according to democratic procedure shows that the Ruler is not unduly worried.

He has a State Police, under a British commander, and the force, recruited largely from Omanis and other expatriates, is efficient. Internationally Bahrein's main ally is Saudi Arabia, and King Faisal's lead in oil matters is followed without question. Relations with the Shah of Iran, who waived his claim to the islands, are good. There is no doubt that if Bahrein should ever be actively threatened from within or without the Saudis and Iranians would quickly intervene.

Kuwait has an area of 600 square miles and a population of over 700,000, but over half a million of these live in the capital, the rest being spread over the arid, infertile hinterland. It has a National Assembly, with an elected Opposition, and is well-governed. It has enjoyed great wealth from oil revenues since soon after the Second World War and took the lead in the Arab Development Bank — which seek to help the less-endowed Arab States and are well-equipped with experts to vet applications. Some $225 million, on easy terms, have been lent for this purpose.

The main oilfield, at Burgan, is operated by the Kuwait Oil Company (BP and Gulf) and the efficiency of the installations is very high indeed, placing Burgan among the most productive fields in the world. A member of the Opposition in the Assembly pointed out, erroneously, early in 1972 that at the current rate of extraction the proved reserves would be exhausted in 12 years, and for this and other reasons it was decided to level off production at 3 mbd instead of increasing it to 4.5 mbd, which would be possible with the existing installations.

The profusion of villas in Beirut owned by rich Kuwaitis indicates that there are doubts about the continuing stability of the State. There are perhaps two reasons for this. In the first place Iraq has an old claim to the whole of Kuwait territory. In 1961, Kuwait called in British help against a threatened Iraqi invasion and the USSR supported Baghdad's claim. Later, in 1963, Iraq recognised Kuwait's independence, but in 1972, after a request for a loan was refused, Iraq began military manoeuvres on the Kuwaiti frontier. The problem then was Iraq's demand for permission to lay a pipeline through Kuwaiti territory to form an outlet to the sea for the USSR's exploitation of Iraq's North Rumaila oilfield. Iraq also asked for possession of two islands which guard the approach to the new naval port at Umm Qasr, which is planned to provide the USSR with a facility at the head of the Gulf. These requests were refused and on 20 March the Iraqis moved across the frontier, using Russian-built tanks and armoured cars. The attack was repelled, partly with the help of British aircraft and Saudi land forces. But the issue remains.

The second reason is a question of the make-up of Kuwaiti society. Dr. R.M. Burrell wrote:

> And another problem within Kuwait, and one which could lead to serious unrest, is the issue of citizenship. At the moment, less than half of the residents of Kuwait are citizens of that State, and not to have citizenship is to suffer decided economic disadvantages. The most recent salary increases for civil servants, for instance, applied only to those employees who were

Kuwaiti citizens. Non-citizens also labour under the disadvantages of not being able to own, buy or sell land or build a house. They are also liable to expulsion from the country at 24 hours notice. Citizenship can be acquired by those who are not Kuwaiti-born, but only after ten years of residential status. The problem is compounded by the fact that many of the non-Kuwaitis hold important jobs within the bureaucracy, the oil industry and social services and, at the moment, cannot be replaced by adequately trained Kuwaiti citizens. (*The Persian Gulf*, Washington 1972).

Why are there so few adequately trained Kuwaitis? The same position is found in all the Gulf States, although Bahrein and Iraq are to some extend exceptions. But while there is an understandable delay in recently developed countries in producing an educated and trained generation of white-collar and skilled workers, there is no excuse in Kuwait. Here there has been prosperity for 25 years; State education in primary, secondary and technical schools is free; and there are free clothes, meals and books, as well as grants for older pupils. But only 43 per cent of the teachers are teacher-trained, and well over half are foreigners, who tend to dislike their job because they can be directed from school to school without regard to where they live, and because discipline is difficult to maintain when the pupils are much better off than the teachers and any complaint by an influential parent may result in arbitrary dismissal.

The trouble is that in the traditional Arab way of life higher education was not regarded as essential for men or desirable for women, and Kuwaiti parents still cling to old traditions. The result is that in the schools, and even more so in Kuwait University, teaching is left far too much in the hands of Palestinians, Egyptians, Indians and Pakistanis who are under-privileged and resentful of their status, and who may be tempted to lend themselves to subversive movements.

Kuwait society is still based very much on Islamic culture and custom, and although the Ministry of Education is liberal-minded and has made great strides in its literacy campaign, it acts under the watchful eyes of the traditionalists, who sponsored a recent decree that will ban all coeducation, even in private and foreign schools. This means that almost twice the number of teachers will be required, and further aggravates the problem of Kuwait's emergence as a modern State. Lying between Iraq and Iran, which are thrusting themselves into the modern world and are both formidably armed, Kuwait depends for security on its unpredictable neighbour, Saudi Arabia, and has some reason for its fears for the future.

Saudi Arabia is in a class by itself. It is nearly as extensive as India, but the population lies somewhere between five and seven million. Owing to lack of water, only 0.20 per cent of the land is cultivatable by normal methods. It might be possible at the cost of titanic effort, to find means of making the desert productive. (Ironically, it is the Israelis, pioneers of arid area agriculture, who could be of most help here.) But this operation would be fruitless unless the Bedouin could be educated at the same time to find an interest in tilling the soil and settling down. So education must be given priority, and there is no disagreement about that. New schools are continually being opened and the first task of the educational system, to achieve literacy, is well under way. But the infrastructure of educated Saudi Arabians is still insufficient to bear the weight of the social and economic evolution of the country. Hence, as in other Gulf States, the need to employ expatriates.

In fact, although the ruling family has enjoyed considerable wealth since the late 'forties, the country still lacks not only an educated middle class, but roads, railways and industries needed for development and even sufficient armed forces to defend its frontiers and patrol its shores. All these needs are being fulfilled, but at a rate which is in no way commensurate with the enormous accretion of wealth. The Saudis, therefore, require skilled help from abroad, and are fully aware of this. But there are some aspects of life in Saudi Arabia that impede a massive inflow of foreign technological and cultural influence, and these have a bearing, indirectly, on the problems of security and stability with which we are concerned:

First, it must be remembered that Saudi Arabia has never

been ruled by a foreign power, so that Western ideas were not introduced, as they were in the other Gulf States, during the period of British colonial administration. The people remained, and still are, proud, independent, deeply religious and bound by ancient traditions. These often conflict with modern ideas and prove an obstacle to progress, although there is a gradual move towards compromise. In the towns the acquisition of wealth has merely preserved the old social pattern, but on a more luxurious scale. In the desert, Bedouin treasure the old values, but are slowly giving way.

Second, there is the stifling effect of a bureaucracy whose stranglehold — according to foreign residents — becomes tighter every day. A British businessman who had a useful and badly needed product to sell blamed bureaucratic obstructionism for the fact that he had to make no less than twenty-three visits to Saudi Arabia before he could sign the contract. (This is one reason why counterpart proposals by consumer countries, readily offered and accepted, often prove extremely difficult to implement to the satisfaction of either side.)

Third, there is a deeply imbedded suspicion of all foreigners. A senior executive of ARAMCO said, "If you want to understand these people you must realise that they have been the target of every con man in the business."

Statements which would not be taken very seriously in Europe, like Senator Jackson's alleged, "Why don't the Arabs realise that the Jews are their best friends?" and Senator Fulbright's suggestion that it might be necessary to call in "the military surrogates Israel and Iran" to sort out the Middle East problem, are mulled over in Riyadh as if they were indications of United States policy. The oil companies are the subject of suspicion. Sheikh Ahmad Zaki Yamani, quoted verbatim in the *Daily Express* of 10 December 1973, is alleged to have said:

> Since ARAMCO is incorporated in Saudi Arabia I, as Oil Minister, have been made a member of the Board. But, that's just show business. It's meaningless. ARAMCO has what it calls its executive committee, and that is where they plan the

real business, where they get instructions from their parent companies in America.

I want to be there. I want to know what is going on and I want to have a say in it. And that is what frightens them most.

The foreign missions engaged in helping the Saudis to train and equip their defence forces are stationed in widely separated areas, and are not encouraged to cooperate with each other. This principle of divide and rule is carried into the military formations themselves; if one, for example, gets tanks, the other gets anti-tank guns. The Army and the National Guard are kept apart, so that should the Army become rebellious the Guard could defend the King. The National Guard is in fact a strong force designed mainly for the protection of the Crown. It is entirely drawn from the Bedouin tribes of the interior, whose Emirs are responsible for recruitment.

There are 15 regular battalions in barracks, regularly on the strength, and in addition each Emir has the obligation to hold 1,000 men trained, armed and ready, so that in case of trouble they can be mobilised immediately. For this service the Emirs are paid handsomely from the King's purse. The men attend regional training schools set up by the British Military Mission to the National Guard. Besides the 26,000 men who form this "Territorial Army" the Emirs could and would recruit more men from their tribes if necessary. As in Jordan, the sense of loyalty of the Emirs and their tribes to the King is regarded as practically unshakeable, and they form a strong deterrent which Subversives no doubt bear in mind.

The Guard was earlier officered almost entirely by well-trained Jordanians (also Bedouin), but when trouble with Jordan broke out many returned to their own country. Saudi officer cadres are being built up, and there are members of the ruling class amongst them, including some of the royal princes. The men in the ranks make good soldiers, and handle tactical weapons well. Their morale is excellent. The Commandant is Prince Abdullah, who is not a claimant to the throne and who would be responsible for order if the King died and there was any confusion over the succession.

King Faisal is a devout Moslem and a hard-working absolute monarch. The administration is run largely by his brothers, half-brothers and sons, with some expatriates in high places and a great many more in the lower ranges. Prince Khalid is Crown Prince. The royal family and the sheikhs make up the ruling class. Many of them have been educated abroad and although some are more Westernised than others they are generally held to be very able, dedicated administrators.

The rank and file of the civil service are held under strict discipline. There is an all-pervading network of informers working for the security service, and criticism of the regime is discovered and punished without distinction of person. A Communist-inspired *revolution* in Saudi Arabia is unthinkable in these conditions, and not least because most Saudis, as good Moslems, are fanatically anti-Communist. There is always the possibility of a plot, but while the Royal Family maintain their present cohesion and — more importantly — their lines of communication to the people, no plot is likely to succeed.

The National Guard has two other functions: to protect the State against the intrusion of guerrillas from Iraq and South Yemen, and to watch over the security of the ARAMCO installations. For both tasks there is a requirement for more helicopters since the distances are great and by the time troops are moved up to the trouble area by wheeled transport the attackers may have disappeared back across their own frontiers. But as in all armed forces there are many claims for the more sophisticated aids, and it is a question of pilots as well as planes.

There is a standing threat from the People's Democratic Republic in South Yemen (PDRY). Both the Russians and the Chinese have given aid and arms to the PDRY but the Chinese are the chief sponsors of this revolutionary National Front, which has its official aim: ". . . to take up its historic responsibilities *towards the Arabian Gulf and all areas of the Arabian Peninsula* for the elmination of the international imperialist and reactionary forces". (Our italics.)

The Saudis regard this threat from a small (1.5 million inhabitants, 90 per cent illiterate) nation seriously, both because of the Great Power backing and because the PDRY, with its capital at Aden, guards the entrance to the Red Sea, which forms Saudi Arabia's western flank. They have supported "armies" of exiled South Yemenis and strengthened the shaky republic of North Yemen with subsidies. In 1972 war broke out between North and South Yemen. Neither side was able to make territorial gains of any importance and in November the two presidents signed an agreement to set up a single Yemeni Republic. . It was soon obvious that neither side was prepared to implement the pact, and fighting again broke out. The question is still unresolved.

The important point is that the Saudis did not take the opportunity of sending in enough troops to enable North Yemen to conquer the PDRY. There are various reasons for this: lack of sufficient trained troops and logistic facilities, hesitation about precipitating a conflict which might escalate, and perhaps fear of the Chinese and Russian reactions. But there is no doubt that the PDRY is a thorn in Saudi Arabia's flesh, and an additional reason for dislike is that the South Yemenis are regarded in Riyadh as atheists. At the moment one hope for the future lies in the fact that the Russians and Chinese are jockeying for position in the PDRY. With its fine port at Aden and firmly established Marxist system it would make an excellent base for an invasion force directed at Saudi Arabia. However unlikely this may seem, the idea is always present in Saudi strategic thinking.

The Saudis are concerned with two other potential threats from outside. Neither seems likely to materialise, but the situation caused by the Arab-Israeli war and its aftermath makes almost any confrontation in the Middle East seem possible.

Iraq is not a Communist State but has received $700 million from the USSR in aid alone and her armed forces are 85 per cent equipped with Soviet weaponry. The anti-traditionalist and anti-monarchical regime and its Ba'athist form of socialism are proving viable, in spite of the debilitating effects of frequent coups d'etat. The State is developing much more rapidly than Saudi Arabia, although there are serious internal problems. Worst of all, perhaps, in Saudi eyes, Iraq has allowed the USSR port facilities at the very head of the Gulf, far too near Saudi Arabia for comfort. More recently, it was Iraq that defied the conception of Arab unity by continuing to deliver oil after the ban eas announced. It is true that the regime at once nationalised certain foreign oil investments; but let its own interests come first, and proceeded to sell oil to all comers and earn the revenues that it so urgently needs.

Iraq has a large army and air force, equipped with sophisticated weapons. Iraqi agents have been active in Saudi Arabia and in the peripheral States of the Yemens and Oman, and the Saudis fear that if circumstances permitted Iraq would attack them.

The other external threat, in Saudi eyes, is from Iran, the non-Arab State that is the odd-man-out in the Gulf area. There can be no doubt that this fear exists, but it appears to be based more on a deep and traditional mistrust than on practical considerations of power politics. There is some degree of understanding and mutual respect between King Faisal and the Shah, but each is said to have doubts about the stability of the other's regime. In the present situation there must be speculation in Riyadh about what the Shah might do if the effects of the Arab oil policy worsened to such an extent that Western and Japanese economies were in danger of breaking down. It might not matter so much to the Saudis if the Western goose with the golden eggs showed signs of sickness, but Iran needs a constant and increasing supply of eggs.

We should now look at the security of the oil installations, and for simplicity, since ARAMCO holds an almost complete monopoly of the foreign oil business, confine ourselves to that company.

The Arabian American Oil Company is a consortium of Exxon, Texaco, Standard Oil of California and Mobil. The Saudi government also has a 25 per cent stake in the company. It began production in 1938, reached an output of 1 mbd of crude in 1958, 4.5 mbd in 1971 and nearly 6 mbd in 1972 (an increase of 27.5 per cent over the previous year) and was working at the rate of about 8 mbd before the restrictions were imposed. In 1972, 95.3 per cent of all Saudi Arabia's crude oil exportation came from ARAMCO sources, 80 per cent being loaded directly into tankers at the terminal of Ras Tanura. 8.9 per cent was refined at Ras Tanura and 7.8 per cent and 2.9 per cent were pumped through the pipelines to the Lebanon coast (TAPLINE) and to the Bahrein refinery respectively. (All figures approximate.)

In the same year, from these operations, over half the sum of crude and petroleum products went to Europe, 30 per cent to Asia, 6 per cent to South America and only 4.5 per cent to North America. These figures are given to illustrate two main points: (a) the direct and immediate effect of overall reductions in Saudi oil production is far more serious for Europe and Japan than for the United States and (b) the scale of ARAMCO operations, whose output of 8 mbd falls only slightly short of the total oil production of the United States (9.5 mbd) and is greater than that of the Soviet Union (7.9 mbd). We also see the dependence of Saudi Arabia on tankers for the delivery of 90 per cent of its oil products.

ARAMCO has been under increasing pressure by the Saudis to allow greater participation in its policy (cf. Sheikh Yamani's remarks quoted above), and its wish to demonstrate goodwill is shown by the fact that in 1972 the company's expenditure in Saudi Arabia *apart from royalties and corporate tax payments* was 100 per cent up on the previous year, at over $350 million. It has built and maintained schools and technical colleges and model factories; given grants for private industrial enterprises; subsidised health schemes and shown the lead in agricultural development. In return, the Saudis appear to have no wish to nationalise ARAMCO provided they get the inside participation they ask for. It is an open question whether the nationalisation of the company would facilitate hostile action against its installations.

Soviet intelligence services representation (1973)

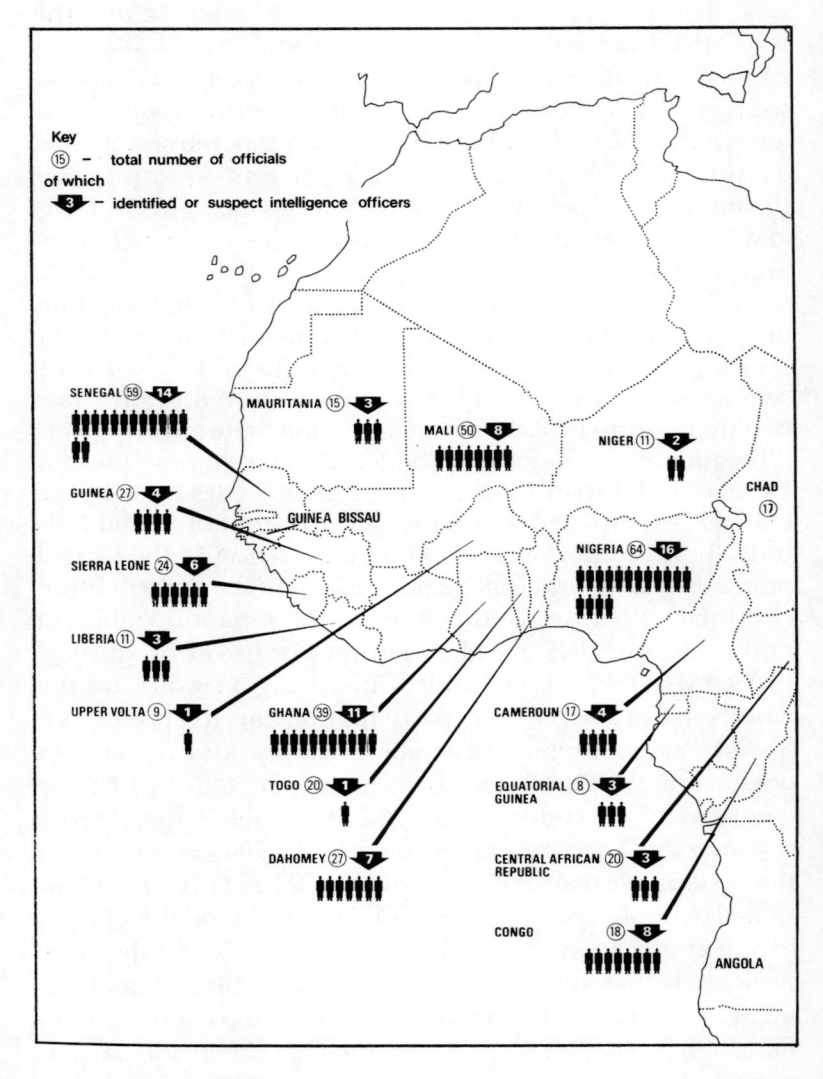

Key
- ⑮ – total number of officials
- of which
- ▼3 – identified or suspect intelligence officers

Country	Total	Intelligence
SENEGAL	59	14
MAURITANIA	15	3
MALI	50	8
NIGER	11	2
CHAD	17	–
GUINEA	27	4
SIERRA LEONE	24	6
NIGERIA	64	16
LIBERIA	11	3
UPPER VOLTA	9	1
GHANA	39	11
CAMEROUN	17	4
TOGO	20	1
EQUATORIAL GUINEA	8	3
DAHOMEY	27	7
CENTRAL AFRICAN REPUBLIC	20	3
CONGO	18	8

It must be assumed that Soviet agents will have been present and active in Mozambique since 1974.

THE SECURITY OF THE CAPE OIL ROUTE

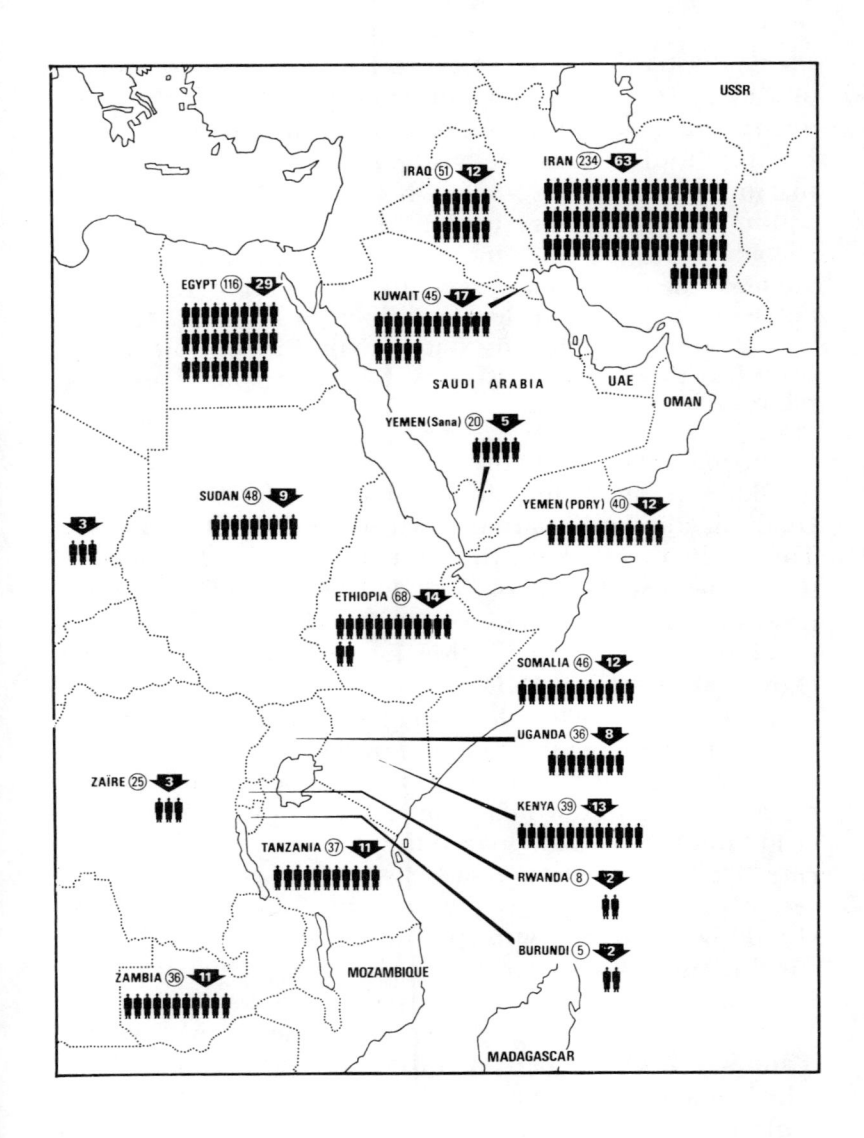

It is impossible, with targets as vulnerable as a pipeline, a refinery, a tank farm or a tanker, to achieve 100 per cent protection against skilled sabotage teams using modern equipment. Plastic explosive and detonators are easy to conceal and every sensitive point cannot be watched all the time. There are portable mortars and launchers with heat-homing heads that can be brought at night within striking distance of the target, and a whole range of small delayed action mines. So far there have been no sophisticated sabotage attacks, and the last two serious attempts to damage the TAPLINE were five years ago. Both were amateurish and had little effect, since the damage is at once registered at the pumping stations and the oil flow turned off before there is any great loss. Even a big pipeline can be repaired in a few days.

The main ARAMCO drillings are to the north and south of Dhahran, opposite Bahrein Island. Across the bay from Dhahran, the headquarters town of ARAMCO, is the Ras Tanura Peninsula with the land and sea island terminals, the refinery, with a capacity of 560,000 bd and gas liquids processor with a capacity of 89,000 bd. From Dhahran a pipeline runs to the refinery at Bahrein, and from Qaisumah the TAPLINE crosses the Arabian desert to the crude terminal 1,000 miles away at Zahrani, near Sidon.

The most vulnerable points are the refinery, where an explosion in a vital part could cause immense damage, and the terminals, from which on an average 5 million barrels of crude and products are loaded into tankers every day. Great care is taken to protect these areas, and the government has recently ordered that security precautions against sabotage should be increased, with specific stipulations. But besides the difficulty of countering sophisticated techniques there is the added danger that a delayed action device might be hidden in, or under, a tanker before her arrival at Ras Tanura. ARAMCO delivers oil to ships flying many flags which often take on part of their loads at the head of the Gulf and call at Ras Tanura to fill up. ARAMCO has no tankers of its own, and this makes the task of ensuring that tankers are "clean" when they arrive at the terminal particularly difficult.

Summing up the security situation in Saudi Arabia it may be well to emphasise that there is a danger of equating the persecution mania of the Saudi officials with threats that may be insignificant or remote. To repeat, there is at present no revolutionary situation, the menaces of PFLOAG and PDRY have not so far resulted in much damage and the fears expressed about Iraq and Iran may be unfounded. The country is vulnerable, however, while its armed forces are still being built up and trained, to attack from outside. Its petroleum installations are also vulnerable, but only to skilled and well-supported operatives.

Iraq is a country of about 150,000 square miles, of which 10 per cent is desert. Of the remainder, traversed by the Tigris and the Euphrates, a large proportion is cultivated or cultivatable, and large sums are being spent on irrigation and planned agriculture. Partly due to the nature of its land, more viable than the arid wastes of the lower Gulf and Saudi Arabia, Iraq has a comparatively advanced society with — for a country of 10 million inhabitants — a good number of institutes of higher learning and a growing middle class. It is on its way to becoming a modern, part-industrialised State, but it still has a long way to go. The Iraqis have a Treaty of Friendship with the USSR (May 1972) and are well armed by the Soviets for defence against Iran, their main enemy. In addition, they are dedicated to the spread of socialism throughout the Arab world, and are cordially hated for it by all the Gulf States.

The country has a 900-mile frontier with Iran. For many years there has been dispute over the channel of the Shatt-el-Arab, which takes the waters of the two great rivers into the Gulf. The quarrel is too complicated to summarize here, the main point being that the channel is still under dispute, and this affects the traffic of the Iraqi port of Basra and the Iranian Korramshahr, both on the channel. However, Iraq now has a terminal at Khor-el-Amaya, 25 miles outside the mouth of the Shatt and connected with the Rumaila oilfield by pipeline. Iran has also provided itself with oil ports outside the Shatt at Kharg Island and Bandar Mahshahr.

Iraq's claim to the two islands commanding the approaches to Umm Qasr, mentioned earlier, still stands. It has offered to relinquish a claim to the whole of Kuwait in return for the island of Bubiyan, which it would use as an oil terminal for a pipeline extending out to sea from the North Rumaila oilfield, and for Warbah Island, to be used as a military base. Iraq appears to have dropped its request for permission to pass the North Rumaila pipeline across Kuwaiti territory.

The Iranians complain of the infiltration of Iraqi spies and saboteurs. It is certainly true that Iraq supports the Khuzistan Liberation Front, which is active in Iran's most south-westerly province. In turn Iraq, probably with truth, asserts that the Shah has armed the Kurds, who form Iraq's most obstreperous minority. On both sides of the common frontier troops are maintained at full strength.

The principal oilfields are at Kirkuk and Rumaila. Most of the oil from the Kirkuk field is pumped by pipeline to Banias in Syria and Tripoli in Lebanon. In 1961, the Iraq Oil Company (B.P., Shell, Compagnie Francaise des Petroles, Mobil and Standard Oil of New Jersey) was forced to give up 90 per cent of its concession area, which included the rich North Rumaila field. In 1969, the Soviet Government made an agreement with the Iraqis to provide a large loan and the technical assistance necessary for exploiting the North Rumaila field, in return for crude oil shipments. Exploitation began in 1972, when another agreement was signed, promising further technical assistance and aid from the USSR. At present the oil is shipped in "small" tankers of 30,000-40,000 tons from Fao, reached by an 80-mile Soviet-built pipeline, but there are plans to build a much longer pipeline to a point on the Mediterranean with a capacity of 1 million barrels a day.

In 1972 IPC was fully nationalized, and in March 1973 the Lebanese Government seized the pipeline branch that connects with Tripoli, and the Tripoli installations and refinery, all belonging to IPC. At the outbreak of the Arab-Israeli war Iraq nationalized the Mobil, Partex and Exxon interests in the Basrah Petroleum Company and later, as a reprisal against Holland, the Dutch interest (presumably 60 per cent) in the Royal Dutch/Shell holding. The Iraq Government now hold all the main sources of oil and gas in the country. At the moment of writing, Iraq's shipments of oil have been halved by the destruction of the Syrian end of the pipeline, but it will continue to load tankers for the Cape Route.

If we turn to the stability of the Iraq regime the record is unpromising, since revolutionary changes of government have been frequent. There is some speculation about the attitude of the USSR to Iraq. In spite of all the public cordiality relations are believed to be deteriorating, owing largely to Iraq's refusal — following Egypt's example — to accept the role of a tied client State. But the USSR presumably needs the facilities it is getting at Umm Qasr, at least until it can establish a proper base in the Gulf or northern Indian Ocean. As for threats to Iraq's oil supply, it is possible that the Palestinian extremists are critical of Iraq's refusal to restrict sales of oil, but so far no threat appears to have been uttered publicly by the PLO or its affiliates.

Iran is 600,000 square miles in extent, with a population of over 30 million. Most of it is arid tableland or salt desert, but the Iranians are thrifty, industrious farmers, and with government advice and aid are developing very large areas of previously infertile land for agriculture and pasture. There is a parallel and very impressive industrial development. The *Economist Intelligence Unit* estimated that by 1980 Iran would be the largest market in Asia except for Japan, since by that time her import bill would be running at the rate of $6,000 million a year. This calculation assumes that the country's GNP will continue to increase at about 10 per cent annually.

Much of the import bill is for military hardware. According to *Flight*, 26 July, 1973, some $3,000 million had already been spent in recent years and an even larger sum would be spent in 1974—75. Iran is already by far the strongest State in the Middle East and its arms are the envy of many European countries — 800 new Chieftain tanks, the first fully operational hovercraft squadron and the largest heli-force in the world, the most modern strike aircraft and ships, up-to-date bombs and missiles. The navy, operating from Bandar Abbas near the mouth of the Gulf and Char Behar, near the Pakistan frontier, will be strong enough to guard the Gulf and its approaches from any attack in "peacetime" conditions. The army will have an overwhelmingly stronger and heavier tank force than the 300 or so T.54s and T.55s owned by the Iraqis. The air force is being more than doubled and will have at least 180 F.4D and F.4E Phantoms and 141 F.52 Tiger IIs from strike action, and 80 F.A/B fighter bombers, as well as aircraft for interception, defence and transport roles. (There is little doubt that the Shah's main reason for taking the lead, at OPEC meetings, in greatly increasing the price of oil was to help cancel off the heavy debts incurred abroad by his purchases of arms.)

The Iranian armed forces, in fact, are strong, modern and well served, and they are obviously greater than required to keep Iraq in order. Gavin Young, writing in *The Observer* of 5 August 1973, commented:

> ... Who are the enemies against whom these huge stocks of military hardware could effectively be used? They don't seem to exist. The West's friends are monarchs. They fear Communist and radical aggression. But where is it to come from? The Chinese Foreign Minister, on a recent visit to the Shah of Iran, publicly embraced his regime. The Russians are friendly with Iraq, Iran's bugbear, but also have good relations with the Shah. No one imagines Soviet fleets and armies churning aggressively about in the Gulf, bombarding the palaces of oil-rich sheikhs, and imposing people's republics in the desert....

The article aroused little comment in Teheran, perhaps because to the Iranians the counter-argument is so obvious. They would say that their intentions are not bellicose but purely defensive, and that they do not necessarily believe that in the long term Soviet and Chinese protestations of friendship can be trusted. Iran has twice suffered take-overs by the USSR and Britain, and does not wish to be taken unawares again. There is a very long frontier with the USSR and in the south a *potential* threat from a Pakistan which might succumb to Chinese influence, from the independent Baluchi movement in both Iran and Pakistan and, even more problematically, from Afghanistan.

There is little evidence that Iran's military build-up is bellicose in the sense of aggression. Although the Shah is primarily concerned with the protection of the tanker route through the Gulf he has said publicly that he would welcome an alliance of all the Gulf littoral States, *including Iraq*, to help police it. He is careful not to exacerbate Arab feelings, and his support of the lower Gulf States is diplomatic and unobtrusive. He would prefer a Gulf from which foreign naval vessels were excluded, and viewed the small USN presence in Bahrein as little more than an excuse which allowed in the Soviet fleet. He would certainly resist, on the diplomatic level, any Soviet proposal to develop their facilities at Um Qasr into a naval base. It is interesting to note that on 7 October 1973, shortly before the outbreak of the war, Iran and Iraq resumed diplomatic relations.

As Mr. Young noted in his article, the armed forces of Iran could turn against the Shah. Although prosperity has percolated through to all Iranians, and there are few parts of the country where people do not point proudly to new evidence of development, the traditional anti-modernist strains in the community are still strong, and occasionally throw up splinter factions of revolt against the new ways. Only five years ago the Shah had machine-guns turned on him, and in October 1973 a plot to kidnap him and his family (and also an un-named foreign ambassador) was allegedly discovered and stopped in time.

Despite this the Shah appears to have complete control. There is no expatriate labour problem, although there are a few foreign advisers. In general, and if we can accept that the Shah has no taste for imperialistic adventures, we can regard Iran as stable within the scope of this report.

The production and distribution of petroleum products in Iran is complicated, but can be summarized as follows:

The national organisation, NIOC, controls all production. There are oilfields at Agha Jari, Marun and Gach Saran, all on-shore. The principal terminal is on Kharg Island, 25 miles from the coast east of the mouth of the Shatt, but there are others at Abadan (displaced as chief terminal owing to the shallow water) and Bandar Mahshahr. There are also three offshore fields, including Feridun in Mid-Gulf. An increasing quantity of natural gas is piped to the USSR from the treatment plant at Bid Boland, and a new pipeline is planned, as well as a new short connection (120 km) between Bid Boland and Ahwaz.

Crude is shipped in tankers from Kharg Island, some of it in Iranian bottoms (the government has ordered 250,000-ton tankers from Japan). There is a plan to connect the oilfields, through Ahwaz, with Iskenderun on the Turkish coast. The cost would be high (about $900 million) but there would be a throughput of 1 mbd which would form a useful alternative outlet for Iranian crude if there were trouble in the Gulf, and also a convenient way of supplying the East European countries with which Iran has barter deals. Iran has a refining capacity of 600,000 bd and the exportable surplus is now shipped through the Gulf.

All oil installations in Iran are given special protection. As far as is known there has been no officially-sponsored Iraqi attack on oil targets. On the other hand the Palestinian Black September Movement is said to have threatened to sabotage tankers, and if they could use Iraq as a base there would be little difficulty in striking at the smaller Abadan tankers that sail through the Shatt. Any Iraqi attempt to cause real damage to the oil installations would no doubt result in immediate reprisal by the Shah's forces who would not — in such an extreme eventuality — hesitate to cross the border. It is therefore unlikely that Iraq would consider such a step.

6. Challenges in southern Africa

The general pattern of Soviet and Chinese strategies in Africa has been described, a closer look is needed at the ways in which they may affect the security of tankers as they enter the channel between Mozambique and Madagascar, follow the coast — not less than 12 miles out to sea for the VLCCs — to the Cape of Good Hope and turn out into the Atlantic, where the traffic divides, westwards for the Americas and, for the European traffic, northwards towards the western coast of the "bulge", and later passing Guinea Bissau and the Cape Verde Islands (CVI).

Soviet thinking about the ultimate attraction of African States into its sphere of influence has changed radically in recent years, largely as a result of setbacks in Egypt and the Sudan, but also because of the growing realisation that African soil is infertile for the seeds of Communism unless it can be given a protracted period of preparation. Hence a slower approach through the development of relations with "bourgeois" governments by aid, trade and diplomacy, in the hope of winning client States. At the same time, partly as a means of denying full control of revolutionary movements to the Chinese, and partly for propaganda effect, the Soviets continue to supply arms to revolutionaries in Guinea and Southern Africa and provide training for them. They also support the campaign for an "anti-colonialist" war against Southern Africa (discussed later in this section.) While competing with the Chinese in a struggle for influence, the Soviets cannot stand aside from an effort which is so clearly aimed at the Western countries that rely on the rich territories of Southern Africa for raw materials.

There is one area of struggle in which the USSR has no competition from China — the Indian Ocean. By increasing its presence to about twenty five warships in the area the Soviets are able to make frequent visits to East African ports and thus pave the way for the use of "gunboat diplomacy" if conditions should favour it. The South Africans, and Iranians are disturbed about this activity, and feel that more should be done by NATO fleets to maintain their "prior presence."

The Chinese have not entirely renounced their ambition to export the Maoist theory of "people's war", despite their failure to provoke such conflicts, and continue to support revolutionary movements with arms and training, but their policy in Africa is at the same time subtler than that of the Soviets and aimed at shorter-term success. There is no lack of evidence from China's official statements that it regards Africa as the key to its world programme. The Chinese have spent more in Africa in recent years than the USSR and United States combined; and Tanzam railway project, linking Dar-es-Salaam with Zambia, is costing them more than the Soviets paid for the Aswan Dam.

Tanzania comes most directly under Chinese influence: there is a very large Chinese work-force of between 25,000 and 30,000 men, both technical and manual, at work on the Tanzam Railway and Chinese military advisers and training officers have attached to the *Front for the Liberation of Mozambique* (FRELIMO). On the island of Zanzibar there are an unknown number of Chinese advisers and "technicians".The Chinese have supplied President Nyerere with fast gunboats, though not yet in large numbers, and training staff. A substantial Chinese presence is virtually assured for several years: the railway has yet to be completed to link Dar-es-Salaam with the Zambian rail network, and after that major work will have to be carried out to increase the capacity of Dar harbour. This work is expected to be carried out by the Chinese — but it is in fact doubtful to what extent Dar can be made a useful port both for Tanzania's own exports and imports for trade with the interior and to cope with the export of Zambia's copper and for its imports.

As for Zambia, the Tanzam Railway is valuable as a propaganda exercise and as an excuse for the continued presence of a large Chinese contingent in southern Africa. In spite of ambitious claims to the contrary, landlocked Zambia is for long going to be dependent on the Zaire and Angola railway systems, with their outlet on the Atlantic at Lobito; and — if President Kaunda continues to regard the Rhodesian frontier as closed — on road transport to Malawi and thence by shipment by the Malawi and Mozambique rail systems to the newly-developed deep-water port of Nacala and to Beira. Although Zambia, like Tanzania, provided bases and sanctuary for anti-Portuguese guerrilla movements its attitude towards these was somewhat ambivalent: it actively discouraged disruption of the Portuguese railway system, having excluded one such movement, *National Union for the Total Independence of Angola* (UNITA) from Zambia because of its attacks on the Benguela Railway; it imports considerable quantities of goods from both Angola and Mozambique, and from South Africa; and President Kaunda is well-aware that Tanzam will not be a substitute for the present outlets.

Zaire, to a greater extent than Zambia, is ambivalent in its attitude to the guerrillas and to Angola. It provides sanctuary for Holden Roberto's *National Front for the Liberation of Angola* (FNLA) in the Bakongo region; it is largely dependent on the Benguela railway for shipping out copper and other minerals through Lobito; it aspires to leadership of the Organisation of African Unity; *but*, it allows a Portuguese Consulate General in Kinshasa (though it operates inside the Spanish Embassy and flies no flag); uses Nova Lisboa as Kinshasa's alternative airport; and is preparing through the concessionaire, Gulf Oil, to pipe out oil from its newly discovered offshore fields south of Cabinda to storage tanks in the Portuguese enclave of Cabinda for export. Transit is easy across the Zaire-Angola borders — though this is not admitted publicly — and passengers as well as freight can use the Benguela railway to Lubumbashi (formerly Elizabethville) if they are prepared to walk across the bridge which links the two countries. Despite critical utterances by President Mobutu from time to time, Zaire must be regarded as a pro-Western State.

Malawi, unlike its neighbours, has slender resources, does not support the terrorist movements and maintains good relations with Rhodesia, Portuguese Africa and South Africa. But it could not prevent the passage of terrorists through the remoter parts of its territory.

It seems likely that China's ultimate objective is effective control through revolutionary movements of Central, as well as Southern, Africa; this, at least, is the impression given by the writings and speeches of its statesmen. But the difficulties are formidable, and the Chinese favour the method of first allying themselves with target countries against a common enemy, and then turning on their allies. Thus, while they court the goodwill of States like Ethiopia and Zaire with diplomacy, arms and technical aid, they keep alive their subversive interests in those same countries. Originally, their plan was to draw together the African peoples through the *Afro-Asian Peoples' Solidarity Organisation* in Cairo, but from 1970 onwards their chosen vehicles have been the OAU, the Afro-Asian bloc in the United Nations (in which African States alone hold 42 of the 132 seats) and "front" organisations established around the world.

The task of inducing the Black African nations to take common action required a cause, and this was found under the banner of "anti-colonialism". Great pressure was brought to bear on Rhodesia, South Africa and Portuguese Africa through United Nations action, and steps were taken which progressively isolated these territories from the rest of Africa and blackened them in world opinion. In 1972 the Ninth Summit Conference of the OAU at Rabat decided that the resources of the Liberation Committee should be used primarily in armed struggle against the Portuguese States. Terrorist attacks were intensified and early in 1974 Guiné's capital, Bissau, was itself a target, while in Mozambique incidents occurred much further south than before.

The propaganda war also reached impressive proportions and is still growing. Its effects should not be underestimated on Rhodesia and South West Africa. Three NATO countries — Holland, Denmark and Norway (as well as Sweden and Finland)—appear to follow the Afro-Asian line in the United Nations, and there is implacable pressure within these countries — and to a lesser extent in others such as the United Kingdom and, the United States — to stifle the growth of normal commercial, political and cultural relations with Southern Africa. The campaign is based on hatred. When over a long period, facts have been constantly misrepresented and "events" fabricated for the mass media, world opinion tends to be based on a whole set of false assumptions, and this process is facilitated by aspects of the South African and former Portuguese administrations, particularly in earlier years, that have lent themselves to criticism by the West. The result is that when the victims speak in their own defence, or ask for objective investigation of charges made against them, their voices are drown by counter-propaganda.

It is important to emphasise the extent to which *news is fabricated*. As far back as 1961 Ghana brought charges of slavery and forced labour against the Portuguese government in the forum of the UN International Labour Organisation. The ILO Commission found that the reports, relating to Portuguese Africa, were wholly unfounded, but the emotive words "Slavery" and "forced labour" remained in people's minds. In recent months two non-events have been given much publicity: the "Wiriamu massacre" and the alleged Caprivi massacre, which was treated with greater scepticism. At least a dozen responsible foreign journalists and political observers have satisfied themselves that nothing like a deliberate slaughter of 400 people, as described in a *Times* article on July 10, 1973, quoting reports by priests, occurred in the area. The only incident of this kind — and this is freely admitted by the Portuguese — was when Portuguese troops, caught in an ambush, rounded on thirty villagers who had betrayed them in to it. This was a criminal act by men provoked beyond endurance, and deplored by the Portuguese authoities, but it was not deliberate. It did not occur either at the time or place of the alleged Wiriamu incident. The following quotation is taken from a paper, *The RSA and the Southern Hemisphere,* by Admiral H.H. Bierman, Chief of the South African forces:

> In the world of today no State can exist in isolation. This applies equally to the major powers. Besides the interdependence of States in the areas of economics, industry and commerce, the power struggle between East and West and the ideological trends, which are no respecters of frontiers, must also be taken into account. The forming of blocks, alliances and trade organisations is not a freak of modern society: these are vital necessities of our time. The viability of a State, therefore, is determined to a large extent by international relations. The RSA, in this respect, finds itself in a particularly invidious

position. Due to our geographic contiguity with decolonised Black Africa, the ethnological composition of our population, and our conservative way of life, we have become the target *par excellence* for the application of double standards on the international level. As a consequence our defensive task is exacerbated by the need to combat this prejudice, and by the exertions required to convince at least Western opinion and Black African States of the sincerity of our intentions and the validity of our policy. This task demands the participation of government and governed alike and this, too, demands volition and sacrifice.

This passage summarises the argument being put forward. It is not aggression and subversion which are the main tools of the campaign to bring down the governments of Southern Africa; it is the use of misinformed public opinion, forcing nations to cut away the international ties, both commercial and political, that are required for the stability and growth of modern societies.

7. Security in southern Africa

Since the Lisbon coup of 25 April 1974, the problems of security in Southern Africa take on an altogether new dimension the complexities of which we cannot deal with in detail here. Only the broadest indication of possible future trends can be dealt with.

The Republic of South Africa (RSA)

South African mineral resources include every raw material vital to modern society, except bauxite and, so far as is known, oil (in commercial quantities). It is a major world source of gold, diamonds, uranium, copper, platinum, chrome, vanadium, manganese, antimony and nickel, and has almost limitless reserves of iron and extensive deposits of shallow, thick-seam coal. There is some confidence among Southern Oil Exploration Corporation (SOEKOR) officials that the chances of finding oil in commercial quantity are good. The oil search has been intensified in the past few years, revealing encouraging signs of deposits off-shore at points all round the coast from

Mozambique to South-West Africa, and more recently, in the cretaceous rock formations beneath Zululand.

The comparative ease and cheapness of coal production made it possible, at a time when there was some fear that the United Nations might impose oil sanctions on the Republic, to set up the SASOL installation near Johannesburg, which manufactures gas from coal, and from gas crude oil in quantities sufficient to satisfy a tenth of the country's requirements. SASOL is a world pioneer in this field, which is of increasing importance at the present time. The SASOL plant, already the largest in the world, is likely to be duplicated. According to a *Financial Times* article of 17 January 1974 SASOL, The South African Coal, Gas and Oil Corporation, has been chosen as consultant for the erection of the first two United States coal-to-oil installations. There is also the large NATREF refinery (in which Iran has a share) at Sasolburg, which produces a third of the Republic's refined oil products.

In another field of special importance at the present time, the South Africans are forerunners in the enrichment of uranium for use in reactors. It is believed that nuclear energy will become commercially available in the Western Cape during the 1980s.

These are some examples of the industrialisation of a country that until recently depended, apart from gold and diamonds, on agriculture for its main exports. It is, in short, a richly-endowed, strong and vigorous State, undergoing an industrial revolution of such dimensions that, if for no other reason, the practices of *apartheid* are being steadily eroded. "Job reservation" is becoming a thing of the past, and the law is flouted with the tacit agreement of the authorities.

The urban Africans are rapidly taking over the jobs previously reserved for the "poor whites", and they are becoming the backbone of the new industries and an important and responsible section of the community to whose wishes the government, willy nilly, must pay careful attention. It is mainly among these skilled and semi-skilled workers, often paid exactly the same rates as whites, and among the graduates of the black universities, that political concepts can grow, but they represent a very small part of the black population, which is mainly rural and traditionally opposed to change. Under present and forseeable conditions the black majority will achieve political power only to the extent that it is granted to them by the whites. This means that a black *revolution*, in the proper sense of the word, is out of the question as long as resolute government is maintained and there is no external interference by the great powers.

There is, however, an internal threat from two black African movements supported by foreign interests and dedicated to sabotage and guerrilla action. These are the African National Congress (ANC), to some extent a cover for the Moscow-line South African Communist Party (SACP), and the Pan-African Congress (PAC), Maoist and led by Peking-trained operatives. Both organisations, although outlawed in South Africa, are recognised by the Organisation of African Unity (OAU), based at Addis Ababa, and have many white sympathisers abroad and in their own country, especially at the universities. These movements have little hope of creating a revolutionary situation because the South African security forces are vigilant, determined and highly efficient, and it appears that the "revolutionaries" are being used cynically by foreign powers to add fuel to the war of vilification waged by the OAU and the Afro-Asian bloc in the United Nations.

There may be another reason: to keep small groups of men, trained and experienced in sabotage, for use against specific targets. This applies especially to the PAC, whose members are organised in cells and include Chinese-trained saboteurs. The activities of these two movements are condemned wholeheartedly by *The World*, a Johannesburg newspaper with half a million black readers, because they prejudice the work of the black community towards improving its conditions. The headquarters of PAC are in Dar-es-Salaam, from which the Chinese direct their subversive operations throughout Central and Southern Africa. If the Chinese decided to threaten the oil route their urban guerrillas could be used for attacks against tankers and port facilities, but so far as is known they have at present no reason to do so.

VLCCs cannot dock at South African ports when they call to discharge fuel, to bunker on the return run from South America, and for repairs. Although there are plans to build two dry docks to acommodate 500,000-ton bulk carriers in the large new industrial port of Saldanha, about 100 miles north of Cape Town, and possibly another as part of the projected Richard's Bay complex, it is still uncertain whether these docks will be used by tankers. At present the only way of dealing with a VLCC is afloat, and outside the harbour. Remarkable repairs have been effected at sea by the Cape engineers. Quite recently, the propeller of a 200,000-ton tanker was changed by ballasting her forward tanks until the stern was well clear of the water, and then using a floating crane to fit a new propeller. Minor repairs can also be made without even slowing down the vessel by transferring technicians and spare parts to and from the ship by helicopter seven hours steaming time before, and seven hours after, she has rounded the Cape. The Court Line Helicopter Service, flying a Sikorsky S-61 which can lift over a ton, carries out this essential task from its base in Cape Town. It combines the repair service with the transport of other requirements of a ship at sea — mail, fresh food, a doctor or patient in an emergency, and sometimes the exchange of crews. Although the VLCCs themselves do not touch land, they depend on this umbilical cord, which cannot function without a stable land base. VLCCs discharging oil use Single Point Moorings (SPMs) at the end of submerged pipelines connecting the buoys with the shore collecting stations. For smaller tankers there are dry docks in Durban harbour (1,200' x 148'), and deep berths in the harbours at Durban and Cape Town. These ports are swamped with traffic, and there are always queues of tankers. But the accelerated programme of port extension has to take into account, apart from the oil trade, the greatly increasing traffic in minerals and general cargo required by the Republic's booming economy. Durban is already reaching a throughput of 30 million tons a year.

During the coming decade there will be no lack of South African ports connected with the tanker traffic, and therefore no lack of potential targets for skilled saboteurs. Pipelines, tank farms, heliports, refineries and SPMs are vulnerable, even when strongly protected; a delayed action limpet mine on the bottom of a tanker awaiting orders to enter harbour is comparatively easy to apply, and deadly in effect.

Mozambique

The Portuguese withdrawal from Africa could conceivably lead to a situation where sabotage attacks are launched against western interests from the shores of Mozambique, Angola and even Guinea-Bissau and the CVI.

In Mozambique the West could lose the use of three fine ports. At Nacala there are facilities for bunkering and discharging VLCCs, whilst the tanker facilities at Lourenço Marques were in the process of being extended by the construction of an off-shore terminal at Porto Dobela to take ships up to 250,000 deadweight (dwt.). There is a small dry dock (115 x 17 m) at Beira, and wharves 2,000 metres long, some with depths of 10 metres.

The new FRELIMO controlled government in Mozambique, which will face grave economic problems may well be tempted to tie her trading pattern to China in return for infrastructural development, in the same way as Tanzania has done. FRELIMO, like Nyerere in Tanzania, is bent upon creating a single-party African socialist state, and since 1972 has relied heavily upon Chinese arms and training in Tanzania. If China achieves any long term paramountcy on this seaboard her influence would, providing present trends continue, be turned against the expansion of Soviet seapower in the area. But this can be of little comfort to those dependent upon the oil route, as it introduces the uncontrollable element of Sino-Soviet rivalry on what is a western lifeline.

In the short term, however, the new government in Mozambique will probably seek to stabilise the frontier with South Africa. Provocation could lead to retaliation; but, more important, Mozambique is dependent upon earnings from miners, working in South Africa, white tourists, freight and harbour dues as well as the future sale of power from Cabora Bassa. No matter whether Mozambique borrows from East or West, the interest, in the first instance, must come from these sources. In the longer term she may succeed, if she still wishes, in substituting them.

Angola

It is still too soon to assess exactly the outcome of the Portuguese coup in Angola where the three contesting revolutionary movements are struggling to maintain a united front capable of filling the newly created vacuum. Here the Sino-Soviet rivalries are more clearly detectable, the Chinese now openly support the FNLA and Russia continues to back Dr. Neto's faction within the MPLA. Rather than a threat to the Cape Route itself, the West stands to lose future oil production from Cabinda, at present exploited by the Gulf Oil Company producing at 135,000 — 150,000 bd (or half the production of Oman or Dubai).

Cape Verde Islands (CVI)

But of much greater strategic importance to the Soviets are the CVI, as a glance at a map will show. Sao Vicente has an important port and naval base at Mindelo. The islands were claimed by the PAIGC government of Guinea Bissau, whose principal support came from Russia and Cuba. But according to the agreement of August 1973 between the PAIGC and the Portuguese Government the islands future will be submitted to referendum; if the population chooses independence from Portugal it cannot be long before the Moscow-orientated Cape Verdeans in Guinea Bissau convince an apolitical population to link up again with their miniature mainland state. In this case the Soviet navy would undoubtedly be interested in procuring for itself facilities at the newly developed harbour, and at the same time being in a position to deny tanker servicing to the West. Needless to say, the strong Soviet allegiance of the Portuguese Communist Party gives Moscow additional influence over the Lisbon Lisnave yards, which offer the largest tanker repair and servicing facilities in Europe.

8. Conclusions

Having concluded a survey on the countries mainly connected with the Route, highlighting their internal political stability and their vulnerability to threats from other countries and from subversive movements, this special report now looks at the situation as a whole. The study group was concerned with *all factors* that may adversely affect the tanker traffic round the Cape, and divide them into categories as follows:

1. Unwillingness by certain producer states to deliver petroleum products to the shippers on the same scale as before, or to increase the deliveries as desired by the consumers. This was discussed earlier under Oil Policy, and it was concluded that in all probability the tanker traffic would nevertheless increase, although not at the same rate as formerly expected.

2. Diversion of the traffic to another route. The only alternative for the Cape section of the traffic is the Red Sea. Here there are two possibilities:

(a) *SUMED PIPELINE*. It was announced in October 1973 that the contract for construction had been won by the Bechtel Corporation of California. The project was to build the line from a point south of Suez to a Mediterranean terminal near Alexandria, 210 miles away. The global cost would be about $540 million, and loans had been offered by American Export-Import Bank and the Kidder Peabody Investment Company in conjunction with the First National Bank, with some Saudi and Kuwaiti support. The first pipeline, with a capacity of 40 million tons annually, would be completed in two years and the twin pipeline six months later. The total capacity would be 80 million tons a year, or 1.6 million barrels a day.

The use of SUMED would require tankers to pass through the Straits of Bab-el Mandeb, commanded by the maverick People's Democratic Republic of Yemen (formerly Aden), and this thought must cause some unease in the minds of tanker owners. (See Appendix IV).

Although there will be discharging docks at the Red Sea terminal of the pipeline it is not expected that they will accommodate the largest tankers, but only those of up to about 285,000 deadweight (dwt).

(b) *THE SUEZ CANAL*. At its present depth of 37 feet the Canal, if re-opened, could take laden tankers up to 70,000 dwt or others up to 120,000 dwt empty. The Egyptian Government has made provisional plans for deepening the channel to 67 or even 100 feet, but in either case it would be necessary to widen the Canal considerably to allow for the angle of repose of the loose sandy banks, and to straighten out some of the bends. The cost of deepening to 100 feet and altering the channel to allow the passage of the very largest VLCCs, fully laden, might prove to be too great, but the 67-feet depth would allow most existing tankers to pass fully laden.

Nevertheless, the considerations which apply to the use of SUMED would be equally operative for the re-opened Canal. Against the obvious advantage of halving the trip time — particularly important with rising fuel costs — there are the dangers of bottlenecks, the hazards of passing close to the PDRY and the question of fees. In general, it seems likely that the reopened Canal will be much in demand by passenger and general cargo vessels, tankers on their way to and from Mediterranean ports and, not least, the Soviet Navy, which could move its fleet units from the Black Sea to the Indian Ocean with far greater speed than at present. It appears very unlikely, unless the area of the Red Sea acquires a new stability, that there will be any great diversion of tankers, particularly the largest VLCCs, from the Cape Route.

3. Instability in the producer States of the Gulf. All the States suffer from revolutionary movements, but at present these activities appear to be contained and there is no evidence of an increase in support from outside. On the other hand, certain Gulf States, for reasons described, are to some extent inherently unstable because of the nature of their societies. International situations of tension, such as the oil crisis which they themselves are causing, can release

forces that may radically change the *status quo*.

4. South Africa. Here again, there is no reason to expect change in the immediate future but the cumulative effect of the world campaign against South Africa is incalculable.

5. Offensive action against oil installations and the tanker traffic. In and just outside the Gulf, the Palestine extremists and the Popular Front for the Liberation of Oman and the Arab Gulf (PFLOAG), if they should decide to interfere with the supply of oil to the West, have many options open to them, and if they remain well supplied with funds and use sophisticated methods it will be difficult to stop them. The fact that Colonel Khadaffi, who has funds to spare, appears to be closely associated with certain Palestinian guerrilla movements, and through his payments to the PDRY may be indirectly subscribing to PFLOAG, is disquieting.

As for the Southern African littoral, the targets are fewer and much more difficult to attack, and in any case the study group knows of no particular reason why either the Soviets or the Chinese should wish to impede the flow of oil. But the OAU has already asked the Arab nations to help them in their campaign against the Southern African States. The requirements of South Africa for Gulf oil, with the exception of its Iranian imports, are small. But should the Arabs decide to finance the OAU Liberation Committee and subsidise the activities of the terrorist movements the "war" against South Africa might escalate dangerously.

Let us take the above factors in turn and see what remedial or preventive action could be taken.

1. The unwillingness of the producers to supply oil in sufficient quantities can be due to:

(a) Political and religious considerations. The religious motive has not in the view of the study group been given enough attention, partly perhaps because experts on the Arab world say, rightly, that most of the Gulf States have never shown very deep feelings about the religious aspect of the Arab-Israeli conflict. They have been obliged to take Egypt's side, for the sake of "Arab unity" and to placate the extremists, but they would not have taken the drastic action of restricting the flow of oil if it were not for the need to follow Saudi Arabia's example, and their own economic interests. But Saudi Arabia is a different matter. It is a deeply religious nation and King Faisal himself is a very devout man. In particular, he has always felt the Jewish occupation of Islam's second holiest city, Jerusalem, to be intolerable affront to the Moslem faith, and to himself as the guardian of Mecca. This point was made strongly to the rapporteur by one of the royal princes shortly before the outbreak of war:

> We know that the Americans have internal reasons for wishing to support Israel, but they can at least put pressure on her to accept the United Nations Resolution of 1967, and particularly the terms for the future of Jerusalem. The situation in the Holy City is of particular concern to my country, more so than to other Arab States, but the Americans have refused to support our case even on this question, which cannot be of such great importance to them. If they could take a firm line over Jerusalem, it would be a very good beginning. This is a matter about which His Majesty my father feels very deeply indeed.

The same point will no doubt have been made to the American Secretary of State, Dr Kissinger; but when this Report went to press, it remained to be seen whether the Israelis would be induced to make concessions on Jerusalem at the Geneva peace talks. The main political factor in the restriction of the oil flow is the Arab-Israeli conflict, but in the post-war period there will be other problems.

No one visiting the Gulf can ignore the frequent references by Arab officials to the "untimely withdrawal" of British forces east of Suez. They remember bitterly that three months after being given an official assurance that the military presence would be retained as long as it was requested, the unilateral decision was taken to withdraw it. Offers of funds by Arab rulers to maintain the *status quo* were refused, and after three years, in 1971, the last British troops left. However small their presence had been, it was a protection against the cold winds blowing from outside the

Gulf and the smaller States still feel the lack of it. It is too late to revert to the former position, but greater attention might be paid to showing each one of the Gulf States that Britain is deeply interested in its stability. It is a question of forming *closer* official and diplomatic ties, and *treating the Arabs as friends.*

Friendship is of great importance to the Arabs, as was shown by the dismay caused in Saudi Arabia by their worsening relationship with the US during the early part of 1973. The Saudis could not understand why the Americans should appear to be acting without regard for their long-existing friendship. Why did they have to *veto* United Nations' resolutions condemning Israel? Surely they could have abstained. Why did they not make some gesture during the nine months before the conflict began, to show Israel that it could not have everything its own way? Did they prefer Israel as a friend to Saudi Arabia?

(b) Economic Motives. The question of how to convince the producers that oil need not necessarily be worth more if left in the ground has been discussed, in which it was shown that international procedures might be necessary to protect the banking and investment of oil revenues. These revenues are already being used in participation in oil operations and "downstream" investment such as refineries, petrochemical industries, tankers and even, as in the agreement signed in July 1973 between the National Iranian Oil Company and the Ashland Oil Company of New York, in a chain of foreign service stations.

Negotiations going on between the U.K., France, Japan and other main consumer countries on one side, and the producer States on the other, to effect exchanges of oil for machinery, other goods and technological know-how are an important development; but there is a limit to what can be spent on industrial and agricultural development and even the building up of armed forces. According to unofficial estimates quoted in *The Times* (14 January 1974), the redoubled oil prices mean that the annual oil income of the Gulf States is now running at $100,000 million, against $30,000 million before the October war, and Saudi officials in the Oil Ministry expect their country alone to draw $20,000 million from oil revenues in 1974. If the rocketing increase in Middle East oil production which preceded the war (16 per cent over 1972) is repeated, even partially, it is the Saudis, more than any other country, who will reap the benefit, and their oil income will rise to levels far in excess of anything they can absorb in normal development.

Some formula may be devised by which international banking authorities might guarantee or underwrite major Arab investments abroad, but such investments would attract interest which itself would have to be invested. There is however the possibility of embarking on projects which would require very heavy capital investment but be slow in providing an income return, for example, the development, on Arab soil, of nuclear and solar energy. (The Arab leaders appear to welcome the prospect of alternative sources of energy, and interest has been shown both in Riyadh and by D. Atiqi, the Kuwaiti Oil Minister. The argument is that oil can earn more when it is used for purposes other than burning, e.g. the manufacture of petro-chemicals, plastics and fertilisers, and the Gulf States are in a position to furnish the huge capital costs of nuclear research and development.)

A further possibility, on the same grand scale, could be the development by Saudi Arabia of the Red Sea brines. Along the Great Rift in the sea bed, at a depth of 500 feet, there are upsurges of brine that well through the earth's mantle at a temperature of 250°F. They are extremely rich in some of the rarer metals, and the ultimate gain from their their exploitation could be reckoned in billions of pounds sterling. So far as we know, a method of extracting the metals has not been found and here, again, is scope for the profitable investment of oil revenues.

But if all such forms of investment fail to absorb the astronomic earnings of the major Gulf States there will remain only international action to prevent a continuing crisis in world money markets. It is no use asking the Gulf States to restrict expansion because, as we stated earlier, the West requires more oil — very much more — not the same quantities as before. The greatly increased supply required during the next six years, at least, will be forthcoming only if consumer and producing nations can be brought to work together.

2. Diversion of the tanker traffic to another route. This has already been discussed and the study group has no useful "recommendation" to make.

3. Instability in the Gulf States and Oman. All the Gulf States, including Iran and Iraq, would benefit from an international agreement between them which would guarantee mutual aid in cases of attack or subversion, encourage defence forces to practice collaboration in international agreement between them which would guarantee mutual aid in cases of attack or subversion, encourage defence forces to practise collaboration in international defensive manoeuvres, provide for an exchange of intelligence (which could also be used for counter-subversion operations), resolve the old differences about frontiers and — most important of all — maintain a close control over funds given to Palestinian movements. This may sound Utopian, but the dependence of all the States on one commodity, of world importance, and their need for Western technical assistance, is a bond that might bring them together. Certainly it is in the interests of the consumer nations to help them to do so in every possible way.

4. Southern Africa. The main problem, as we have shown, lies in the future stability of these countries. South Africa, Mozambique, Angola and Rhodesia form, together with Malawi, Zaire and Zambia, an economic bloc, and are largely dependent on each other for communications and trade. Yet, of the three "black" nations, only Malawi maintains diplomatic relations with the others. It is, in the view of the study group, the pressure of the Chinese-dominated OAU and the Afro-Asian minority in the United Nations that forces Presidents Mobutu and Kaunda, neither of whom is a Communist or in other senses a revolutionary, to adopt their present attitudes to the "white South". As far as Western nations are concerned there is a strong need for better information about the countries of Southern Africa. This can best be obtained by high-level fact-finding

missions, able to spend all the time necessary in the countries concerned, travel extensively, and later publish authoritative reports. There is reason to believe that South Africa would welcome such visits, as indeed they welcome any visit by an open-minded foreign observer.

The next aim should be to help South Africa to improve its relations with Angola and Mozambique. This is feasible, as Dr. Banda of Malawi has shown, but it can be greatly facilitated if the problems and achievements of South Africa can first be ventilated, instead of being smothered, as at present, by a world campaign of misinformation.

W.A.C. Adie is Senior Research Fellow at the Department of International Relations at the Australian National University at Canberra. A graduate of Oxford University, he is co-author (with L.C. Goodrich) of *A Short History of the Chinese People*, his most recent visit to the People's Republic of China having taken place in the summer of 1973. He is widely regarded as one of the most experienced and authoritative commentators on international affairs in the West, especially with reference to China and the Far East.

W.A.C. Adie

STRATEGIC PROBLEMS OF THE INDIAN OCEAN AREA

The interests of the Great Powers

THE US and USSR have common interests, but man no common border; the local confrontations of their proxies and protegés can become cumbersome for their global policy, which is increasingly concerned with China, Japan and Europe. China and USSR have both common interests and a highly militarized border, but except for occasional clashes their conflict has been displaced and cooled into a struggle for influence first in the Third World and then in Japan and Europe (designated by China as the Second Intermediate Zone).

The Indian Ocean comprises most of the Third World, which both Peking and Moscow see as a most important arena of their struggle, and in which they have both sought to enlist allies against each other under the pretext of helping them emancipate themselves from the political and economic hegemony of the West. In recent years Peking has increasingly denounced the joint hegemonism of the capitalist world market under the U.S. and what Krushchev called the "economic system of socialism", centred on the USSR, and has encouraged small and middle powers to emancipate themselves from this dyarchy.

In almost identical language, the militarists of Japan once proposed to emancipate countries of Greater East Asia from the hegemonism of Britain and America. Especially since the fall of Marshal Lin Piao and his "united fleet" of militarist plotters in September 1971, China's handling of international relations has increasingly stressed diplomacy rather than "people's war". But Premier Chou En-lai stressed in October 1971 that the era was still one of "armed struggle" as well as of negotiations. This riposte of the Premier's to President Nixon's categorization of the era as one of "negotiations" only should draw our attention to certain historic and domestic factors which have given Mao's China a means of action in international relations which was not developed, or not to such an extent, by militarist Japan and the other combatants in World War II, nor by the protagonists of the Cold War which succeeded it. This is the "international united front" exploiting existing "contradictions", conflicts and, in the maximum programme, armed struggles. Now the Cold War is merging into "hot diplomacy", or rather, hot business and "resources diplomacy" in some parts of the world; but in at least one part of the Indian Ocean area — the Middle East and Africa — armed struggle is still on the agenda, and has enabled Peking to make political gains at the expense of Moscow and the other extraneous powers.

On the global level, Nixon expected "a safer world and a better world if we have a strong, healthy U.S., Europe, Soviet Union, China and Japan, each balancing the other, not playing one against the other, an even balance". His Guam doctrine moved away from the Dullesian policy of containment and rollback by the "creative counter-pressure" of a U.S. alliance system and towards "creative ambiguity", benign neglect and a spontaneous, multipolar balance of power, the counterpressure to China being provided by the USSR, and *vice versa*. Before Stalin's death, the USSR began moving away from the bloc concept towards Krushchevian "peaceful coexistence and economic competition" and recently reached the stage of Dullesian pactomania, the minimum programme always remaining defence of the Revolution (read: of the ruling group) and the maximum programme, its advance. (Read: inclusion of new territory in Soviet sphere of influence.) Beginning with trade and aid (often military, as required by local conflicts) Moscow has sought to promote such "regional co-operation", "economic integration" and "division of labour" as would facilitate signing of bilateral treaties (as with Egypt, Iraq and India) and eventual construction of a collective security system to render China innocuous by encircling or including it. The Subcontinent is the key to this system, which basically aims to preserve the status quo.

China, on the other hand, has recently moved away from the para-military approach associated with Lin Piao and back towards the Soviet style methods ascribed to Liu Shaoch'i — conventional state-to-state diplomacy, trade and aid; but its overall economic disadvantages vis-a-vis the superpowers have been compensated by certain special conditions in Africa, which have enabled Peking to reap great political advantages from maintenance of the militant posture and supply of what it had — surplus railway-building capacity, armaments and other wares less sophisticated than those available from the USSR.

This is one reason why Africa has been the key to China's system of the "International United Front", which has not sought basically to maintain the status quo by either an alliance system or a power balance but to generate enough counterpressure to change it. To the extent that China has joined the U.N. and otherwise achieved greatly enhanced world status, it has already broken out of the status quo — the superpowers' encirclement. But the position of its rulers is still in many ways insecure. In spite of the military origins and aspect of the Peking regime, China's militancy in Africa and the Middle East must now be regarded as an opportunist tactic in the framework of its policy of mobilizing a "third force" at the U.N. and in the Third World, to enable it better to manoeuvre between its powerful neighbours — the USSR, which constitutes both a military and an ideological, internal-security threat — and Japan. Japan is a threat both in concrete terms as an investor in (and so potential ally of) the USSR as well as an extension of "U.S. imperialism", as a long-term competitor with China for raw materials and some markets and ideologically as a giant Taiwan, armed with sugar-coated cannonballs of the bourgeois lifestyle. Of these two threats Moscow's is probably perceived as major but decreasing while Japan's is becoming more concrete. This is why China's support of EEC is probably aimed at Tokyo as well as Moscow.

In order to understand the importance of the Indian ocean in the U.S. — Soviet — Chinese global power game and in their subgames played at each end of Eurasia with Europe and Japan we need some historical perspective; it is also necessary briefly to consider the problems and policies of the diverse and divided countries of the area which have in the past invited the intrusion of the outside powers, and those congruent interests of the latter which may now require them to try and impose some new "pax" upon it. In anticipation, we should note at this stage that although the Indian Ocean has been of marginal importance for the US. (except for deployment of deterrent missile submarines) it is already regarded as of major importance for Europe and Japan and its energy supplies are expected to become increasingly important for the U.S. itself.

Peking is already exploiting potential U.S. - Soviet competition for Middle East, especially Gulf oil. Citing American press reports, the Peking Review notes that by 1980 the U.S. was expected to import up to fifty per cent of its oil from the area which was already shaping up as an area of rivalry between the two superpowers. The U.S. Committee on Defence Production said that in 1972, twenty-six per cent of oil needs were imported, but by 1985, fifty-five per cent would be imported. The U.S. naval authorities cited above specifically adduced this situation as a reason for increased naval activity in the Indian Ocean. While cogent arguments can be marshalled against the idea of crude Soviet interdiction of these supplies, one should note that the companies engaged in extracting and transporting Middle East oil represent ninety per cent of the estimated U.S. $2.2 billion invested in the region (excluding Israel); the $1.4 billion p.a. revenue from these interests (nearly all of which is repatriated to the U.S.) is of major importance for the balance of payments.

Against the background of the world energy crisis, Moscow's pipeline diplomacy both in the emerging triangular relationships with Iraq and Europe and with Siberia and Japan must be borne in mind; land communications as well as the "sealanes" are important, though liable to attract less attention for historical reasons.

The Indian Ocean

The Indian Ocean area is neither economically nor socially coherent, nor are many of the states in it. Leaving out Australia and South Africa it is poor, both in terms of present income per capita and in terms of relations of population to natural resources. The societies are predominantly peasant (subsistence farming) while much of the soil is infertile and has inadequate rainfall. Where this is not the case it is overpopulated.

No country or likely grouping of contiguous countries in the area contains the combination of resources on which the industrialisation of a major power such as the U.S. was based. Only India offers the economics of scale that many types of manufacturing industry require. From this industrial weakness, military weakness inevitably follows.

Such enclaves of modernity as exist within the peasant mass of a given country — *e.g.* plantations, mines, industry — tend to be insufficiently integrated with it though they play a disproportionately large part in the economy and provide a large percentage of government revenue. Similarly, trade is mainly with countries outside the region. This divorce between the real, backward countryside and islands of modernity oriented towards the way of life of advanced countries creates manifold social and political problems. In spite of rising expectations the gap between the outback (mofussil, ulu, bundu, etc.) and the Afro-Asian city is expected to increase; so is the gap between those cities and the "world city" of Europe, America and Japan.

Apart from relative deprivation in material terms, the real cause of the instability strategists fear is to be found in the sphere of psychological deprivation — *e.g.* the frustration of a subélite, of young people educated above their parents' level but without satisfactory employment and of detribalised new shanty-towndwellers experiencing the industrial revolution. Above all, the rapidly rising proportion of adolescents in the population of many countries has already given cause for alarm. These tensions contribute to the prevalence of xenophobia and communalism in the guise of nationalism, and symbolic development led by a repainted traditional elite or a military dictatorship in the name of socialism.

The "principal contradiction" (in Marxist terminology) is expressed in the form of "fissiparous tendencies" — communalism or local nationalism exacerbated by religious differences and institutionalized up to the State level by the existence of Islamic Pakistan, and now (paradoxically) secular Bangla Desh. The post-war split has enabled outside powers to pick proxies in the area and inside factions to pick protectors, resulting, broadly, in the line-up of Pakistan with U.S. (against Communism in the U.S. intention but against Indian in Pakistan's) and later with China (both against India and the USSR) and now India's line-up with the USSR against what is perceived or projected as a joint U.S. — Chinese threat. But as in the Middle East Moscow has diversified its options by dealing with Egypt's rivals, Syria and Iraq, so in the Subcontinent it has supplied arms to Pakistan as well as to India and tried as far as possible, in view of the prime commitment to India, to push "regional economic integration and division of Labour" of both countries so as to link them with the Soviet economic system, via Afghanistan and build them up, with Bangla Desh, to contain or balance China. This balance must be thought of as ultimately military in the sense of preventing redeployment of Chinese troops to the northern Soviet border, as well as on the level of more intangible factors such as economic power, Afro-Asian leadership and influence in the U.N.

This is the thrust of Article 6 of the 1971 Friendship Treaty which calls for greater co-operation in the scientific technical and economic fields, including trade and transport. After conclusion of an agreement to set up a Commission on Economic, Scientific and Technical Co-operation to co-ordinate Indian and Soviet planning, the pro-Soviet newspaper *Patriot* launched the idea of linking India to CMEA (the Moscow inspired Council for Mutual Economic Assistance, or COMECON) which was rejected by Mrs. Gandhi. While the latter has sought to balance Soviet influence by mending fences with China, China has now shown eagerness to reciprocate although it would appear to be in its interest. I was officially told in Peking that this was because of the hostilities between India and Pakistan and the subsequent retention of Pakistani prisoners of war by India. With Soviet political influence strong but lacking the same lasting economic base (*e.g.* a grain surplus) as American influence, a Chinese political counterbalance and a non-American Western economic counterbalance is indicated.

With right-wing elements joining Mrs. Gandhi's ruling party from the splinter Congress group her dependence on the Communist Party (CPI) has been reduced and Moscow has accordingly encouraged the CPI to step up agitation against the Government, leading the Editor of the *Times of India* to speculate that Moscow was seeking to end its "more or less complete identification" with New Delhi. This "identification" seems to have originated from Soviet hopes of taking over the idea of regional economic co-operation which was mooted by India during the period of China's Cultural Revolution, and building on it Brezhnev's edifice of Collective Security.

Though both schemes aimed at security, Mrs. Gandhi's approach stopped at what President Suharto of Indonesia calls "national resilience" and even persuaded the Russians to suggest that China could join while they, for their part, were clearly interested in military and naval factors as well as the strategic aspect of an industrial and communications buildup. Moscow has pushed its own version of Collective Security on three levels — economic (co-operation), political (treaties) and military, the latter being the submerged part of the iceberg. Initially it was necessary to concentrate on the economic stage, so as to draw in Pakistan. Suspecting these implications, perhaps, Peking commented "the Indian reactionaries" efforts to form an anti-China alliance have to be carried out under the camouflage of economic co-operation .... Indira Gandhi made a big effort to peddle the idea of "regional co-operation" in Asia, pretending that the countries of South East Asia should stand together and help one another in becoming economically strong in order to deal with the so-called threat from China.

The 1971 crisis enabled Russia to move onto the political level with India implementing plans laid in 1969, but the continuing hostility between India and (West) Pakistan made it necessary to revert to the level of economic co-operation in order to bypass this obstacle. The 1969 scheme for an overland route linking the USSR, Iran, Afghanistan, India and Pakistan was revived in April, 1972 in the form of a "rail trunkline", in an *Izvestiya* article which clearly linked the application of "co-operation" in Asia to Moscow's plans for "integration" and "Finlandization" of Europe. Meanwhile Article 9 of the Indo-Soviet Treaty lays down that "In case either of the Parties is attacked or threatened with attack (they) shall immediately start mutual consultations with a view to eliminating this threat and taking appropriate measures to ensure peace and security for their countries". It has been suggested that Indian anti-submarine warfare forces might therefore be used against U.S. Polaris/Poseidon submarines in the Arabian sea or bay of Bengal. India is reported to have offered facilities to Soviet warships at the submarine base of Vishakapatnam, where Soviet naval aid is concentrated, and at Bombay, Cochin, Mormugao (Goa) and Port Blair in the Andaman islands, from which ports Soviet missile submarines could operate against China.

The Indian Navy has been supplied with Soviet submarines and other equipment, giving rise to the problem of distinguishing a Soviet-manned Soviet warship from an Indian one. In spite of much fuss about Soviet "bases", similar to the furore over Diego Garcia, official investigations have concluded that "the USSR is seeking only limited berthing and recreation facilities in the region although undoubtedly it would wish to keep its options open for the future".

A recent study of Soviet naval policy concludes that:
The presence of the Soviet Navy in the Indian Ocean is so far not large enough or supported on a scale sufficient for far-reaching naval objectives. It probably represents a combination of flag-showing force and area-familiarization detachment orientated (a mix of SSM, SAM and ASW ships) to an anti-Polaris and/or anti-carrier role, with the additional political objective of securing denuclearization of the Indian Ocean.

It would be ironical if the naval option recommended to India by K.M. Panikkar in 1945 were exercised on behalf of the USSR instead of in connection with Britain and its natural successor the EEC. But India has in fact strongly supported the proposals for neutralization of the Indian Ocean and its recognition as a zone of peace made by the Lusaka Conference of non-aligned countries in September 1970 and by Mrs. Bandaranaike of Sri Lanka (Ceylon) at the Singapore Conference of Commonwealth Heads of Governments in January 1971. One of the reasons for Ceylon's preference for such a solution is the role of the Indian minority within the island's multiracial structure, which forecloses the option of regional security arrangements implying Indian hegemony.

While advocating the peace zone as an ideal, Sri Lanka has in practice followed a "more the merrier" or balancing policy towards involvement of big powers in the region. While maintaining better relations with China than with the USSR (there are not many Overseas Chinese in the island), it has extended a welcome to U.S. naval forces also. Persistent reports about Soviet or Chinese hopes for a base at Trincomalee are officially discounted and it is pointed out that when Soviet forces got a foot in the door on the ground of defending the Government against the JVP rebels, they were soon seen off again by Mrs. Bandaranaike. It should be noted in passing that the JVP revolt is a classic example of the effects of miseducation on top of failure of the economy to expand as rapidly as the population. As an official publication put it "the educated have been trained for jobs that the economy, such as it is, does not need".

In South East Asia, Malaysia has adopted something similar to Ceylon's theory and Singapore, to its practice; in both cases largely because of ethnic factors.

South East Asia

The principal contradiction consists in Balkanisation and minority divisions, the problem of the overseas Chinese reaching in effect up to the State level in Singapore which is regarded increasingly as their metropolis and a sort of Israel surrounded by the Malay-Muslim world, all the more suspect because of its potential links with the super-Israel, China, which is a power in the area although outside it. With the end of the Vietnam war declared and perhaps realizable in fact, some observers in the area, especially Singapore, fear that the North Vietnamese communists rather than China will be a seriously destabilising element in the region as they seek hegemony in the peninsula to strengthen their State against China, the hereditary enemy.

From the point of view of the great powers it is a vital link and transit area like the Middle East, of major importance for the USSR and Japan, as well as possessing great, partly untapped natural resources. On 16 November 1971, Indonesia, Malaysia and Singapore issued a statement that the Straits of Malacca are not international straits, though fully recognising their use for international shipping in accordance with the principle of innocent passage. The implication of this, taken with a 12 mile claim for territorial waters, is that the Sunda and Lombok straits also could be denied to the Red Fleet, cutting communications between the Baltic and Black Sea and Vladivostok for about six months of the year. China's vociferous support for measures taken by several countries to extend their territorial waters may be due to the fact that over one hundred straits which were high seas when territorial waters were three miles, become territorial waters when they are twelve miles, the

Malacca straits being among them.

Malaysia also has a neutralization concept, applying to South East Asia only. Since the idea was launched by de Gaulle as part of his Grand Design in 1964, with the corollary of recognizing and co-opting Peking as guarantor, the aftermath of the 1965 *coup* in Indonesia and the end of Konfrontasi enabled, indeed required the Soviet leaders to reappraise their policy towards Malaysia, and *vice versa*; the decimation of the Indonesian Communist Party imposed on Moscow tactics of "united front from above" with the Government instead of from below, but attempts to make "fisheries" agreements, etc., as the price of renegotiating outstanding debts made little progress in face of the anti-communism and pragmatism of the military rulers, unconcerned to reactivate the rusty Soviet-supplied Navy incurred by Sukarno and concerned with their Overseas Chinese and other factors of disunity. While the military in particular are concerned for the possible effects of "playing the Chinese card" on internal security, civilian policymakers tend to see some value in it, if only to "follow the trend". Sujatmoko, for example, has written "China may well have a stake in an increased self-reliance of the countries of the region. At some point, she may even come to see the utility to her of some non-ideological form of regional co-operation, aimed at enhancing regional strength and self-confidence. And with some strength of the imagination it may not be entirely inconceivable that China at some point will see the advantage to her of a system of interlocking external balances in the region which, in combination with the increased capabilities of the countries themselves, would amount to an effective neutralization she may not even be asked to guarantee."

For a while over the last few years China was placing its stones in Moscow's back yard, the Middle East; during the late 1960s the Soviets and other Eastern European countries reciprocated by opening diplomatic relations with Malaysia and Singapore and developing trade or other contacts with Thailand and the Philippines. Soviet naval activity was also increasing and Soviet divisions were massing on China's frontier. All this added up to the "creative counterpressure" or shock treatment which the present writer saw in 1966 as a prerequisite for China's "joining the world" and of which President Nixon wrote in October 1967. This set the stage for an approach similar to that of the Shah in the Gulf — seeking to give both Russia and China a stake in one's stability. At the same time, regional co-operation was developing with the creation of ASPAC (June 1966) and ASEAN (August 1967), the Asian Development Bank, etc.

As Adam Malik, Indonesia's Foreign Minister, pointed out, the three basic options for the countries in the region are neutralization, alignment with one or a combination of Powers or, preferably, development within the region of "an area of indigenous stability, based on indigenous sociopolitical and economic strength". President Suharto has chosen the latter option, which he calls "promoting national resilience of the respective nations".

> If this can be enhanced to regional resilience, then we can be sure that stability and security of this region can be preserved by the nations of the region themselves. However, the concept needs time to materialize ... Through the national resilience of each country in this S.E. Asia region the concept of neutralization of S.E. Asia will possibly be realized in its true sense and not merely be neutralization dependent on the big Powers.

A Soviet Economic and Technical Agreement was signed with Malaysia on 4 October 1972. The Soviet commentators drew the analogy with Iran and made it clear that the intention was to move from economic to political links, and thence to the maximum programme — Collective Security giving the USSR military facilities or ties of the Egyptian-Indian type predicated on some sort of containment of China.

However, the Malaysian idea of regional security is naturally not part of a global scheme connected with the talks for mutual balanced force reductions in Europe,

European security Soviet style, SALT and détente with the U.S. and so forth; it is closely connected with considerations of internal unity and security arising from the disparity between economic and political power of the local Chinese community and the shadow cast by China itself over the region. As Tun Abdul Razak put it, "the China issue is the centre of Malaysia's foreign policy".

How to give China a stake in the stability of multi-racial Malaysia? On the one hand, direct dealings by the Malaysian Government with Peking are expected to head off possible development of "Chinese chauvinism" orienting loyalties outside the country, and to deprive its extreme expression, the jungle Malayan Communist Party guerrillas, of Peking's support. On the other hand, direct monopolistic trading by the Government Trading Corporation, PERNAS, with its Chinese counterpart should help to prevent the economic strength of the local Chinese and their links with China from having a disruptive effect.

Tan Sri Ghazali Shafie proposed neutralization at a preparatory Conference of non-aligned countries at Dar es Salaam on 17 April 1970, but later three steps were listed as necessary even before the superpowers and China could in practice guarantee it, not to mention any purely indigenous balance. First each country must set its house in order, develop a "greater sense of regional consciousness and solidarity" and "demonstrate that our activities and policies do not adversely affect the basic legitimate interests of the major Powers". Failing this, Malaysia continues to rely on the Five-Power Defence arrangement until it can be phased out.

This is understood by policy-makers in Indonesia and Singapore, who have privately expressed doubts about the feasibility of Malaysian-style neutralization. Singapore would naturally regard exclusion of outside Powers as implying a Malay/Muslim hegemony and encirclement which would be dangerous in the event of radicalization or revolution in Indonesia or Malaysia. It therefore inclines to the "more the merrier" approach on the ground that the big Powers cannot be kept out of the area anyway. As Lee

Kuan-yew put it "we must ... be realistic and expect there will be considerable competition for influence among the major Powers over this region." What is not clear, Singaporeans say, is why China should help Kuala Lumpur solve its communal problem; Malaysian spokesmen told the present writer at the end of 1972 that Chou En-lai's reaction had been favourable; he said that the overseas Chinese were regarded in Peking as daughters who had married out of the family; before Tunku Razaleigh's trade mission to Peking in May 1971 the pseudo-clandestine Chinese radio "Voice of the Malayan Revolution" said that the Razak clique's so-called guarantee for the neutralization of South East Asia by the big powers was "only a product of the Nixon Doctrine". But the confusion of signals may have been due to the power struggle in China revealed by the fall of Lin Piao.

After seeking for a time to maintain a common front on the related questions of establishing diplomatic relations with the People's Republic of China and "neutralization" of the region, during the first half of 1973 the five ASEAN states broke ranks, with Malaysia out in front. Though expected to recognize China first and soon, at the time of writing (July 1973) Kuala Lumpur was not in such a hurry to receive an actual Chinese Embassy. In spite of much talk since November 1971 about enlargement of ASEAN and the neutralization of S.E. Asia, practical problems such as the Sabah issue between Malaysia and the Philippines blocked progress. Another factor may have been a certain conceptual confusion about the meaning of neutralization as distinct from neutralism, non-alignment, neutrality, de-militarization, disarmament, declaration of "peace zones", pacifism, etc. It is worth pointing out that the term "neutralization" refers to a precise status which can only be based on an international agreement, of which the prime example is Switzerland. Its status as a neutralized state in both peace and war was laid down by the Act of Paris of 20 November 1815 signed by Austria, France, Great Britain, Prussia and Russia as guarantors of Switzerland's perpetual neutrality and the inviolability of its territory. In return, the neutralized state is obliged to eschew foreign military aid, bases, etc. or any kind of alliance. For this reason, Switzerland is not even a member of the U.N.O.

On the other hand, the status of a neutral or non-aligned state (*e.g.* Sweden) is self-proclaimed unilaterally and may operate only *ad hoc* for a given conflict or period of time: there is no legal obligation by outside powers to guarantee or defend it or by the "neutral" state to avoid outside military involvements in peacetime. Naturally, practising politicians have not always observed these fine distinctions: for example a Malaysian Minister wrote that

> Neutralization . . . refers to the act which brings about a state of neutralism, (which) refers to the foreign policy of a state, either alone or in concert with other states, in time of peace.

Neutralization in the proper sense could hardly be acceptable to Indonesia, or to Singapore, apart from the tie-up with China which begins with the valid argument that it must be an outside guarantor but then may slide over to the notion that China must be involved in the area diplomatically and in other ways or even ultimately as a member of some new regional grouping.

Labour Governments in Australia since December 1972 have shown a tendency to associate the ideas of changing the regional security arrangements and of neutralization and "peace zones" in Asia and the Pacific with the active involvement of China in the region; but soundings along these lines made by the Prime Minister, Gough Whitlam, were not welcomed in Jakarta or New Delhi. Indeed, during my talks in Peking in June 1973 in became perfectly clear that far from insisting on precipitate withdrawal of British Commonwealth or even American troops from the region, Peking would prefer them to stay rather than be replaced by the Soviets. Even Chiang Kai-shek and the U.S. troops in Taiwan have their function in preventing the establishment of an independant Taiwan sponsored politically by Moscow and economically by Tokyo as makeweight of their co-operation in Siberia.

The Oil Factor

After initially scoffing at the idea of neutralization, the Soviet Union switched to trying to use it as a starting point for development into its own collective security scheme, presenting the Malaysian proposals in *Izvestiya* as "repercussions" of Brezhnev's. The Soviet Government's organ was unusually explicit in stressing the relationship between collective security and the "social liberation of the Asian countries and the liberation of their economies from the overlordship of foreign monopolies". The help given by OPEC to Iraq and Syria when they nationalized the Iraq Petroleum Company was quoted as an example. This line must be considered in the light of probable Soviet plans to import Middle East oil and supply it to Europe by pipeline via the dying Caspian fields, while selling its Siberian crude to Japan — thereby giving the Capitalist world a stake in the stability of the Soviet regime. China also advocates anti-Western moves by OPEC in the framework of its general line on tariffs and trade ("emancipation", etc. preached at the time of the UNCTAD conference in 1972). According to some petroleum affairs specialists, unless recent speculation about Sino-Japanese co-operation to develop vast deposits in the China Sea proves correct, China will also need Gulf oil before the end of the century, in competition with Japan and the other developed Powers.

At present China regards itself as self-sufficient in oil production — because its consumption per capita is extremely low. The USSR and CMEA (COMECON), on the other hand, are already suffering from an increasing gap between Soviet production and CMEA requirements, which makes it inevitable that Moscow should solicit help from both Japan and the U.S. in developing the Tyumen oilfields in Siberia and the necessary pipelines to the Pacific coast, as well as developing Iraq as its window on the Gulf. If only to offset the political effects of these economic linkages, China must logically keep alive the interest shown by petroleum circles in both Japan and the U.S. in developing its offshore oil, though it probably has no intention of allowing any direct foreign participation in drilling or production. In accordance with its new technology policy, China also plans to expand motor transport, agricultural mechanization and petrochemical industry.

In an interview with me, a senior official of the Ministry of Foreign Affairs in Peking played down the possibility of China's developing oil exports in order to pay for the large amount of modern technology it has been talking about with foreign corporations, though the informed sources considered petroleum the most likely asset available. The Chinese official said that supply of the 200,000 tons of low-sulphur crude already sold to Japan had created rail transport and other problems; development of the oil would take time and it would not run away. However, this would only provide Japan with up to three million tons of crude per annum — a fraction of the requirement. The U.S. State Department discouraged the interest shown by U.S. firms in deep water offshore drilling, for which only they are considered to have the technology, because the waters concerned are disputed between North Korea, and Taiwan, or between Japan and Taiwan, China and Vietnam, etc. It is preferred that Canadians should go in, and it happens that in 1972 Chou En-lai himself showed interest in Canadian offshore petroleum technology; a twenty two man mission headed by the Deputy Minister of Fuel and Chemical Industries visited Canada in October 1972. However, in spite of all this activity and China's reduction of oil imports from the Middle East, Albania and Rumania over the last few years, the continuing, importance of these sources cannot yet be discounted. The Soviet Union, for its part, has sought to link the requirements of its own energy crisis and pipeline diplomacy to the broader issues of collective security.

The Moscow visits of the Shah of Iran and Tun Abdul Razak, the Malaysian Prime Minister, were used by Soviet commentators towards the end of 1972 to support claims that the collective security idea was catching on and that "Peking's attempts to hamper relaxation of tensions in Europe (*i.e.* support for E.E.C. and doubts about the Security Conference) could only do serious damage to the security of Asian nations as well".

For good measure, Russian propaganda asserted that "for the Chinese leaders the national liberation movement is important to the extent that they can use it for the attainment of their Great-Power ambitions. When the interests of the movement came into conflict with the power aims of the Chinese leadership, then the movement is pushed aside without ceremony." Conversely, as I mentioned at the beginning of this study, a senior Chinese offical stated that the Social-imperialists (Russians) were more dangerous than others (U.S.) because they used so-called communist parties and self-styled leftists to try and subvert and control other countries.

Nevertheless, the net result of the penetration and/or introduction of Soviet power and Chinese power into the Indian Ocean area in order to counterbalance each other is the increase of influence which one day might again be temporarily and tactically united.

Even in the short term, the prospects for neutralizing or pacifying the region do not look promising. While the U.N. set up a committee in December 1972 to study the implications of declaring the Indian Ocean a zone of peace, on 20th March the U.S. activated its communications station on Diego Garcia and both superpowers went ahead with plans to deploy more "undetectable" nuclear submarines with longer-range undersea-launched missiles (the Soviet 5,000 miles missile and the U.S. Trident system). What called world attention to the Indian Ocean "power vacuum" was the increase in visible Soviet naval activity from March 1968, closely following the then British Government's ill-advised advertisement of its intention to withdraw from East of Suez. But this naval presence is not as important as the Russian economic, political and military involvement on land around the periphery, in such forms as great engineering and land communications projects and proxy use of local armed forces, as once practised by the British Raj. Incidentally, British presence is still not inconsiderable and may, with the French and other concerned Powers other than the superpowers, including regional powers such as Iran, form the basis of a common approach to some aspects of security in the area. The Soviet Union's activities there are part of its global attempt to extend its influence and implement the foreign policy of a superpower, not merely a land-Power confined to Eurasia. Competition with the People's Republic of China on many levels is an important part of this plan, and the Indian Ocean — containing most of the Third World — is a major theatre of Sino-Soviet competion. Opening of the Suez Canal would transform the situation to the advantage of the U.S.S.R.

The Peoples Republic of China has provided a few naval craft to Tanzania and Ceylon but so far has rather successfully competed for influence with the USSR in the area without "showing the flag" in the conventional manner, partly because it has been more able and willing to exploit local "people's wars" as well as winning the confidence of suitable Governments with aid on very "soft" terms. This is the principle of walking on two legs, or, as Lin Piao put it, "the locomotive of revolution runs on two rails". Japan has won economic influence and is involved in schemes for improving communications in Africa, for example, which superficially resemble those of China; China has for several years been denouncing Japanese investment, etc., in Africa most vehemently. However, Japan has tended to be identified only with conservative rather than insurgent forces in the continent. It is expected that some of Japan's raw material requirements will increase by three hundred per cent in the coming decade; as is well known some ninety per cent of her oil requirements come from the Middle East and essentials such as copper and zinc also cross the Indian Ocean from Africa.

The U..S. has interest in the area primarily because of its importance to Europe and Japan; however, the energy crisis is upon us already; whether or not anything comes from the proposals for a special relationship between the U.S. and Saudi Arabia to meet the former's astronomical needs, the U.S. interest in "stability" of the Ocean area must increase.

But what is "stability" and what are the threats to it? I

attempted to answer these questions in a paper of February 1970 on possibilities for regional security in South East Asia. Clearly, politicians and naval staffs, for example, perceive different problems and propose perhaps inapposite responses reflecting the means by which their respective apparatuses can prove they are "doing something" (*i.e.* something quantifiable) about it. What is usually meant by stability in the many seminars, conferences, etc., I have attended on such subjects over the years is simply safe conditions for trade — not political and social stagnation, which in the end endanger them. The dangers in the area are not so much from Great Power interference: war on their scale has become too destructive and, more important, too expensive even to prepare, so that politicians on each side may regard each other as allies in the fight to cut down the budget demands of the military. If the big Powers are too strong to fight, the small ones are, by their very weakness, lack of cohesion and balkanization likely to be the cause or scene of all kinds of destabilizing violence, ranging from delinquency, organized crime, piracy with or without political cover, riots, guerilla warfare and full-scale replays of World War II tank battles and air raids.

When it dawns on governmental committees and similar bodies that the military response is the easy, but wrong way out, the conclusion may all too often be that what tons of bombs cannot do, tons of PL 480 wheat or "massive acid" will do. The next stage of sophistication is reached when experience shows that such aid and modernization in general is profoundly destabilizing and in fact has been responsible for much of the unrest in the post-war era which has been blamed on communist subversion or neo-colonialist oppression, according to standpoint. The experience of Ceylon, Madagascar and many of the other countries of the region shows that apart from the well-known effects of the population explosion and failure of economic growth to keep up with it, a major source of unrest is the maladaptation and excessive cost of Western-style educational systems and the impossibility of finding jobs for graduates of the system once they have got through it.

Experiments are being made in Indonesia with new methods of village education and to develop a new life-style not dependent on Western-level consumption. In the end such indigenous initiatives may prove to be more important for the stability of the area than any made by outside Powers. Meanwhile, on the level of what Governments can in practice deal with, the multiplicity of relations in the "mandala pattern" which is emerging from the end if bipolarity is going to make it increasingly difficult for Chancelleries, Trade Departments, etc., to follow what is going on, and far more to make informed decisions about problems across the multicentred and centrifugal world.

Lessons for Australia

The original conception of this study excluded developed countries of the Southern hemisphere — Australia and South Africa — because of their presumed stability, military and economic strength. South Africa was briefly mentioned because of the race and guerilla issue and the increasing acceptance by world public opinion that it is more heinous for Africans to suffer indignity at the hands of white racists than massacre at the hands of black tribalists. The accession to power of a Labour Government in Australia (and in New Zealand) and the decision of the former to reduce defence forces, on the assumption that there will be no "threat" to the country for twenty years or so, changes the situation in the eastern part of the Southern Hemisphere to a considerable extent. From the Chinese point of view, as Chou En-lai remarked, Australia is the "gateway to the South" — that is to say, to the access via South East Asia to the Indian Ocean.

The conclusion that no identifiable threat can now be forecast was reached after due deliberation by specialists concerned, against the general background of what is commonly seens as the *detente* in international relations, or the end of the cold war. It is interesting to note that Peking vociferously rejects the notion that SALT, the Nixon pilgrimages and the like, imply a *detente:* on the contrary, it warns that the Soviets are more dangerous than ever, and advises noncommunist countries in public and in private to keep up and expand their defence capability; in this the Chinese Government agrees with Dr. Sakharov, the Soviet intellectual oppositionist who incurred some personal risk to "warn the West against the dangers of *detente*".

On logical grounds, it seems unjustified to reason that since the future is so unpredictable, there is nothing to be frightened of. No easily identifiable threat does not imply no threat, any more than a white horse "is not a horse". On practical grounds, it is obvious that what is meant by *detente* in Europe means the final ratification of Soviet neo-colonial control in Eastern Europe, by which the leadership of the Communist Party of this Soviet Union brings in the West to secure control of what hitherto they were always afraid of losing; what is meant by *detente* in Asia is, similarly, confirmation of China's claim to Taiwan and ratification of other Communist gains which hitherto always seemed threatened and temporary (Korea and Indochina); again, the West is brought in (in the form of U.S. troops in Taiwan, American and Japanese investment, trade with and investment from Europe etc.) to shore up an essentially shaky Chinese government whose internal position, after the Cultural Revolution and Marshal Lin Piao's three attempts to assassinate Chairman Mao, is such that for the first time since 1949 the offical People's Daily reports people keeping "accounts" in anticipation of a change of regime, in order to take revenge when it comes. The uneasy tripartite balance between Chou En-lai, Madame Mao and some of the military is reminiscent of situations in the last days of the Roman Republic, except that for the parallel to be nearer, Octavian should have drowned on the way to Parthia after three bungled attempts to kill Julius Caesar.

Precisely because the simplistic bipolar alignments of the cold war are no more, it is impossible to predict for so far as fifteen or twenty years ahead what will happen in the extremely volatile areas covered in this study, especially in the Gulf, the Indian subcontinent and both continental and maritime South East Asia. The Soviet and Chinese planning staffs, especially naval staffs, cannot but anticipate that their opposite numbers will pursue a forward policy; by the well-known mechanism of self-fulfilling prophecy, each will interpret moves made to forestall the other as evidence of the need to make more moves to get in there before they do. As President Nyerere of Tanzania has astutely remarked, the situation is shaping up like that obtaining when the European powers relaxed tensions between themselves at the Berlin Conference of 1884/85; the British and French, and others, scrambled for Africa and elsewhere to get in first, and then settled things amicably — but it did not greatly comfort the Africans. In the same way, the Soviets offer to protect small and middle powers against alleged Chinese expansionism with collective security treaties, and the Chinese offer to mobilise small and middle powers to resist hegemony by the superpowers, especially Russia; this process is liable to end up, in conjunction with the activities of Japan, Europe and the U.S. striving for resources and markets, in a situation detrimental to the independence of the small and middle powers.

In concrete terms, Sino-Soviet rivalry over the Indonesian archipelago and the Indochinese peninsula (in the old-fashioned sense, including Burma and Thailand) is liable to take advantage of any faltering in Indonesia's progress to try and line up that country; given the delicate position of the overseas Chinese in internal affairs. Jakarta may either follow Kuala Lumpur in trying to fix things with Peking over their heads or move towards the remoter and apparently safer Soviet Union; in that case it is not inconceivable that in a very short space of time a treaty relationship similar to that between the USSR and India, Iraq and Egypt would bring modern properly maintained and manned Soviet warships and aircraft to Australia's doorstep. Even a slight acquaintance with the outlook of Soviet decision-makers, as revealed for example in Krushchev's memoirs, would suggest that they could not fail to take advantage of such a situation if Australia had let her defence forces run down — especially if the argument of "revolutionary defeatism" was being raised in the country. This is the argument that it is futile to arm at all, because no Australian forces would be strong enough to defeat a superpower. The point is not in any imaginary eventual invasion, but in the political climate created by a feeling of powerlessness which would make it possible, indeed inevitable for an outside armed entity (not necessarily a state, but even pirates or terrorists) to dictate terms without even needing to employ violence.

The notion sometimes expressed by spokesmen of the Australian Labour Party that the use of military force in international affairs is somehow archaic, that there are no more colonies in the world except those of France and Portugal, and that talk about communism is "garbage" reveal an extraordinary confusion of mind. Communism is garbage, for sure, but Soviet expansion and the Chinese measures to counter it are not. Military force is being used daily to cow people under occupation in Eastern Europe and various parts of Asia and Africa; the outlying domains of the Tsar and the Manchu Emporer, now incorporated into the USSR and the PRC, are just as much colonies as — for example — Angola and Mozambique, and more colonial than South Africa and Rhodesia which are no longer ruled from the former metropolis. In his speeches to arouse the Athenians against Philip of Macedon, Demosthenes used to say that it was no use speculating whether he was sick, or dead. The way they went on neglecting their defences, they would raise up another Philip to overwhelm them. Today, to confuse no immediate and specific threat with no threat at all is the sure way to create one.

The Chinese may in future become a danger to Australian interests, if only to exclude other influences they fear from this rich and under-populated continent. But in the immediate future their advice to Australia might well be similar to that given by Foreign Minister Chi Peng-fei to Iran on his visit in June 1973: "This country must strengthen its defence forces. For its security, independence and sovereign rights, Iran is taking certain measures to strengthen its defence forces. This is a necessary and understandable measure."

RECENT DEVELOPMENTS AND CONCLUSIONS

THE PROBLEM of writing an account of contemporary history is to know when to stop. Events follow each other with such rapidity that appreciations must be altered and assessments changed. In the last months of 1974, since the various sections of this book were written, the West has suffered a number of political and strategic reverses without the USSR having to move a single soldier. Not long ago, although the danger to Western oil supplies was obvious and the first few faltering steps had been taken to correct this weakness, NATO's position was reasonably secure. Today its flank in the Eastern Mediterranean is in a state of chaos, the Middle Eastern oil producing nations are rapidly becoming major military powers, and the West may soon find itself denied the use of some of the best ports flanking the Cape Route.

The Mediterranean

This study has not concerned itself with the Mediterranean though of course events in the Eastern Mediterranean have repercussions on the Middle East. The fighting in Cyprus in 1974 has considerably affected the whole strategic picture and must therefore be covered.

Greeks and Turks have been traditional enemies since the time of the Byzantine Empire. After the defeat of the Turks in the First World War and the dissolution of their Empire, there was almost a renewal of fighting when the Greeks were expelled from Turkish Asia in 1921. The island of

Cyprus lies only fifty miles from the Turkish coast; seventy per cent of its population is Greek and thirty per cent Turkish. It was only British administration (established in 1878) that kept the peace. In 1960 Cyprus was given its independence being guaranteed by Britain, Greece and Turkey, and the British retaining two sovereign base areas including the strategically important airfield of Akrotiri. The Greek majority under its President, Archbishop Makarios, did not permit the full implementation of the constitution and treated the Turks as second-class citizens. Even so an uneasy peace between the two communities continued until General Grivas, the champion of "Enosis" or union with Greece, returned to the island and the Colonels assumed power in Athens. Grivas went underground and fought against Archbishop Makarios's concept of an independent Cyprus while the Turks looked on uneasily. Twice they nearly intervened but it was not until the Greek National Guard, with the encouragement of the Military Junta in Athens, revolted against President Makarios in the summer of 1974 that Turkey decided to act.

While the Greek National Guard took over the island the President fled to Paphos and was flown out of the island by the RAF. Meanwhile the Western nations talked at the U.N. and at Geneva. Turkey, seeing that no positive action was contemplated, invaded the island, landing at Kyrenia. While talks continued and Greek Cypriots murdered Turkish Cypriots and *vice versa*, the Turkish Army extended its operations until they controlled the North Eastern part of the island nearest the Turkish mainland.

Once again action had succeeded where talking had failed. The Turks obtained what they wanted and said that they would still support the concept of a federalised but independent Cyprus.

The stupidity of having supported the military coup in Cyprus was soon proved by the fall of the Junta and the return of Greece to democratic government. Greece was in no position to attack Turkey; so she took refuge in castigating her European allies for failing to halt the Turkish invasion, and withdrew her troops from NATO. At present it appears that she is following the French example by withdrawing her military forces from the NATO command, but remaining a member of the North Atlantic Treaty. By late 1974 it was still uncertain whether NATO's facilities in Greece, such as the bombing range in Crete, would be withdrawn, and the same uncertainty hangs over the future of the US naval facilities in Piraeus and elsewhere.

The net result of the fighting in Cyprus is that the old enmity between the two NATO allies Greece and Turkey has been revived and that NATO's position in the Eastern Mediterranean has been weakened to a degree that can not yet be fully determined. This, together with the re-opening of the Suez Canal, presents the USSR with a major success in a critical area.

The Soviet Navy is split between three main bases, Murmansk in the White Sea where the most modern ships and nuclear submarines are stationed, the Black Sea which, together with the Baltic, is where Russia's main ship-building and repair yards are situated, and Vladivostok in the Sea of Japan from which the Indian Ocean squadron is maintained.

The importance of Greece and Turkey to the West lies not so much in their military power but in their strategic position, controlling the Dardanelles. In fact the weakness of these two countries in the air is the main reason why the US Navy maintains two fleet carriers in the Mediterranean so as to give the Eastern flank of NATO western air support, including a nuclear capacity.

Under the Montreux Convention of 1936 the USSR is restricted in her use of the Dardanelles and has to notify Turkey each time she sends a warship to or from the Mediterranean. Naturally any neutralisation of Turkey would be a major victory for the Warsaw Pact.

The first Soviet warships were seen in the Mediterranean in 1964. The following year their visit was prolonged, and after the Arab-Israeli Six Day War of 1967 the Soviet-Mediterranean squadron was permanently established and was rapidly built up to rival the US 6th Fleet.

In 1972 its composition was as follows:-

COMMANDER (2 Star Admiral)

ASW FORCE	MISSILE STRIKE FORCE	SURFACE STRIKE FORCE
3 ships	3 ships	2 ships
1 Moskva 2 Kashin	1 Kresta 1 Kildin 1 Kashin	1 Sverdlov 1 Kotlin

AMPHIBIOUS FORCE	SURVEILLANCE FORCE	SERVICE FORCE
4 ships	5 ships	15 ships
1 Skoryy 1 LST 2 LSM	3 AGI (Intelligence gathering) 2 AGS (Hydrographic)	

MINE FORCE	SUBMARINE FORCE	NAVAL AIR FORCE
2 ships	10-12 vessels	30 or more aircraft
2 Yurka	i.e. 2 missile submarines 8 torpedo submarines 2 training submarines	TU 16 (Badger) IL 98 (Beagle) Plus fighters MiG 21, etc.

These forces make a total of some thirty-four; ten to twelve submarines, together with thirty long-range aircraft, operated from Egyptian airfields — a facility withdrawn by the Egyptian Government later that year. This fleet was maintained from the Black Sea; the submarines came from the Northern Fleet at Murmansk. Once the Suez Canal is re-opened, these warships can rapidly be switched to the Indian Ocean instead of having to round the Cape or be detatched from the Pacific Fleet at Vladivostok.

The Gulf

Events in the Gulf have been well covered in previous sections, particularly by the report of The Institute for the Study of Conflict. All that need be added is to point out that the oil states now have enormous (and growing) resources which enable them to purchase the most modern and sophisticated arms. Iran has purchased both Chieftain and Leopard tanks and will probably end by having more than the armies of producing countries, Britain and Germany. Oman has ordered the Anglo-French Jaguar fighter which is only just going into service in the RAF and French Air Force. The US arms industry is supplying both Saudi Arabia and Israel, France is sending Mirage fighters to Libya and Kuwait, Britain and America are equipping the Iranian Navy. This build-up is likely to continue for some years. This enormous concentration of arms in such a strategically important area can surely only lead to an explosive situation in the not too distant future.

The Horn of Africa

The Horn of Africa is one of the areas where the USSR has made her deepest penetration. It is also an area of considerable instability. Most of these comparatively recently independent states have traditional racial or dynastic rivalries dating from before the colonial era. The Somalis await an opportunity to invade Ethiopia's Ogaden and Haud Districts and have designs on the Northern Frontier District of Kenya, in which the overwhelming majority of the population are Somali. The Southern Sudan has been gravely disrupted by warfare between the Arab northeners and Nilotic southerners, and relations between Khartoum and Kampala have been strained over recent years. General Amin, Uganda's President, is unpredictable and has more than once threatened to attack Tanzania. Genocide has been committed on a major scale in Rwanda and Burundi. The French are restless in Djibouti, and across the Red Sea the

People's Republic of South Yemen is in its usual state of chaos and friction with its Arab neighbours. In Kenya, perhaps the most stable country in the area, there could well be a struggle for power once President Kenyatta dies. Indeed, the Horn of Africa, controlling the southern entrances to the Red Sea, is one of the least stable parts of an unstable continent.

A recent report to the US Congress stated that "The USSR therefore has concentrated most efforts in Somalia, South Yemen (formerly Aden) and, to a lesser extent the Yemen Arab Republic, where permanent base rights would bolster their abilities to dominate the Red Sea passage. In recent years they have deepened the roadstead and modernised quays at Hodeida, developed Berbera where SAM batteries defend the port, and erected tank farms at Berbera, Kismayu and Mogadishu. Aden reportedly has a Russian harbourmaster. In addition both countries possess airfields ideally suited for reconnaissance flights and shore-based fleet support, which, if in Soviet hands, could help counterbalance US carrier air power."

One of the key personalities in this area was Haile Selassie the Emperor of Ethiopia, who relied on considerable US military support and equipment. Though the head of the most ancient of the world's remaining Kingdoms, he took a prominent part in the work of the Organisation for African Unity. Now his army has rebelled, his personal staff, friends and advisers are locked up and his own future is uncertain. General Aman Andom, who seemed to lead the original *coup*, has since been executed himself; what has happened may well ignite an explosion in the Horn of Africa which could lead to further Communist exploitation.

As yet few in the West appear to realise the shift of power in the whole area that has taken place since the Second World War. Then the West controlled Egypt and the Suez Canal, the Red Sea was an allied lake, and in the Gulf Britain was the dominant power able (and willing) to crush rebellions in Iraq and Iran. Today Egypt veers from the USSR to the U.S.A. and back again; the Canal, once reopened, is far more likely to be controlled by the USSR than by the West; and the Red Sea is a Russian lake from which air reconnaissance can be mounted over the eastern Indian Ocean.

Central Africa

As shown in earlier sections, the Portuguese had virtually won the war in Angola and until 1971 achieved considerable success in Northern Mozambique. The weak spot was the Tete District of Mozambique where the FRELIMO guerillas had penetrated deeply. However, the Cabora Bassa dam project was on schedule and its completion in 1976 would, as FRELIMO themselves admitted, have been a decisive blow to their hopes. It appeared that only two events could defeat the Portuguese, the assassination of Dr. Banda and his replacement by a pro-FRELIMO leader in Malawi or a failure of will in Lisbon.

As we now know, an unusual combination of circumstances caused Lisbon to give in. The young officers, especially those serving four years conscript service, plotted revolt; their action was sparked off by a book of political reflections written by General Spinola, Portugal's war-hero recently returned from Guinea. Spinola wanted greater emphasis on "hearts and minds" operations, rather than on actual fighting; he believed that the majority of Africans were on the side of Portugal against the terorists, and hoped for an association of self-governing states linked together in a form of Portuguese Commonwealth that would include Brazil. This, as I found during my visits to Angola and Mozambique, was in fact the future desired by both blacks and whites in these countries, who resented the centralisation of bureaucracy and of business in Lisbon. Indeed Prime Minister Caetano was slowly moving along these lines when he gave both Angola and Mozambique full Statehood (*i.e.* internal self-government) in 1973 with legislatures containing a majority of non-whites. Unfortunately, however, the reactionary President Tomas insisted that General Spinola should be retired, and a half-hearted *coup* in Spinola's support misfired. This was sufficient to arouse the establishment in Lisbon and led to arrests and repression, which in turn sparked off the officers' *coup* of April 1974.

The young officers chose as their figure-head General Spinola, who assumed the Presidency. It soon becamse clear that the new President had to contend not only with young officers who had very different ideas as to the future from those he had advocated in his book, but with Socialist and Communist politicians who returned from exile. The Communist Party, having long been underground, was soon seen to be the best organised political party in the country and, while appearing to decry strikes and back the Government, it made certain that its members took over organs of local administration throughout the country. The suddenness of the revolution and the dismantling of the autocratic regime that had ruled Portugal since the 1920s reduced the Right to chaos. The Centre had never had much support in Portugal, and parties of the Left proliferated.

The seemingly impossible then happened. The new Portuguese Government arranged for Mozambique to be handed over to FRELIMO — in the teeth of the opposition of the Macua, the largest tribe, and of the majority of the white population. The process of hand-over was being enforced by Portuguese troops. This policy was not that of Spinola but of the Communist and Socialist parties of which his scratch Government was substantially composed. In September 1974, Spinola resigned, in open dispute with the Prime Minister, Colonel Goncalves. General Costa Gomez, a soldier of political sophistication but uncertain convictions, assumed the presidency.

Whatever the outcome, it now seems certain that Mozambique and in due course Angola will be ruled by a predominantly black Government which will be anti-capitalist and anti-West or, at the best, non-aligned. This in turn means that the West can no longer rely on the important ports of Nacala, Beira, Lourenço Marques, Lobito or Luanda, while the future of the strategically placed Cape Verde Islands is uncertain. All these flank the Cape Route, and while their neutralisation would be a blow to the West, their use by the USSR could be a disaster.

Nationalism and Neutralism

As has been pointed out in previous sections, many newly independent African nations have run the full circle of political coups and indeed are now starting their second round. In English-speaking Africa for example, the Westminster Parliament provided well balanced independence consitutions protecting minority races or tribes. These were soon torn up; one party became dominant and suppressed the others; one man then became the dictator, and in many cases his abuse of power led to the only nationally organised force taking over in an Army *coup d'etat*. Army government is seldom effective, so that eventually party politics are again permitted and the whole process is repeated.

In spite of this instablity and of the ineffectiveness of the Organisation of African Unity, African nationalism is a growing force from which all the ex-colonial powers have retreated. In its early days it received much support from the traditionally anti-colonialist United States and today it gets overwhelming support from the U.N. where the Afro-Asian nations virtually control the General Assembly.

Both the Russians and the Chinese have exploited this anti-Western feeling, and, as no Western nation except Portugal has been prepared either individually or collectively to stand up to this pressure, the West has been in continual retreat, its friends and allies being packed off one after another. The withdrawal of the US in Vietnam and the use of the oil weapon by the Arabs have intensified this pressure, which may soon be focused on South Africa and Rhodesia. Later it could be turned on Australia and New Zealand, Brazil or the Argentine, until the Western world is forced back to the North Atlantic when the final blow can be struck against a West deprived of most of its essential raw material.

CENTO and SEATO are virtually non-operative as defensive shields; socialist Australia is running for cover, and the five-power Commonwealth force in Singapore may soon be wound up. Taiwan has been abandoned; the Indian sub-continent is in a state of disruption; China uses the Law of the Seas Conference to try to close international straits, and is resisted by the USSR for obvious reasons.

Only NATO remains, but in NATO countries public attention is focused on Central Europe, where the spirit of "detente" prevails as expressed by the conferences on European Security and Co-operation and on Mutual and Balanced Force Reductions. People forget the flanks, Northern Norway, Denmark and Iceland, where Soviet propagandists are busily at work. Perhaps even more important, the Mediterranean flank is now in disarray due to Greek-Turkish tension. The true southern flank of NATO (though outside the NATO area) — the Cape Route — is neglected. As reported in earlier sections, the NATO service chiefs are only too aware of this danger. Even the NATO politicians in the North Atlantic Assembly are at last agreed that some limited action should be taken, in spite of the strong anti-apartheid feeling in Scandinavia and Holland, which has nothing to do with the strategic issues involved, but is exploited continuously by all the organs of the ultra-left.

The NATO Navies have great difficulty in protecting their primary responsibility, the Atlantic north of the Tropic of Cancer. The Royal Navy has been pared to the bone and further drastic cuts are proposed by the present British Government under Harold Wilson; the US Navy has been reduced in size from 1,000 ships in 1968 to 514 today, and though the French Navy is increasing, the Soviet Fleet is still the most rapidly expanding navy afloat.

The Indian Ocean

The expansion of the Soviet Fleet is particularly apparent in the Indian Ocean. Each contributor to this volume has drawn the conclusion that this endangers the security of his own country — the U.S., Britain and Australia — and of the West as a whole. This situation will last as long as the

Western world depends so heavily on Middle Eastern oil.

The first Soviet deployment into the Indian Ocean took place in 1968 and 1969, when fifteen ports, from the Andaman Islands to Mauritius, were visited. Since then the USSR, in contrast to the Western Powers, has maintained a permanent squadron of surface warships and support vessels in the area. This includes cruisers, guided-missile destroyers or frigates, and submarines. Since 1971, as has already been shown, this presence has been increased to a maximum of some thirty ships. It is true that Brezhnev failed to secure home port facilities in India or the Andaman Islands during his 1973 visit, but the Soviet Navy has docking and bunkering arrangements in several strategic locations, including Singapore, and is surveying a number of potential sites. These range from Chittagong in Bangla Desh to Umm Qasr in Iran as well as the Red Sea ports already referred to. Port Louis in Mauritius provides logistic support, and anchorages exist off the Seychelles, the Chagos Archipelago and the coast of East Africa.

In contrast Britain maintains three frigates and sometimes one submarine at Singapore, and the United States one depot ship and two destroyers at Bahrain. Notice was given to the American Government during the Yom Kippur War of 1973 by the Government of Bahrain for the US to quit these facilities, but it has not yet been implemented.

Excluding Singapore and Simonstown, which are no longer British nor today even bases in the full sense of the word, the nearest British support must come from the British Isles, some 8,000 to 10,000 miles from key points in the Indian Ocean. The nearest U.S. base is at Subic Bay some 4,000 to 6,000 miles distant from the critical areas.

The Soviet Fleet is at present faced with the same problem, Vladivostok being 5,000 miles from Aden and the Northern Black Sea bases being 11,000 miles distant. However these latter distances will be cut by some seventy per cent when the Suez Canal is re-opened, whereas the steaming time from the Atlantic seaboard of the U.S. will be reduced by only twenty per cent. The USSR would therefore gain considerable peacetime advantages.

This emphasises the importance of Diego Garcia which would offer logistic support, air cover and reconnaissance to the allied navies if properly developed. It was therefore reassuring to hear President Ford supporting the expansion of facilities in this British island where the U.S. established a joint communications centre in 1968.

It is also of interest to note the growing Chinese attention towards the Indian Ocean. They believe that however great the difficulties, the USSR will develop an outright challenge to the Americans for supremacy in both the Mediterranean and Indian Ocean and they hope to benefit from this maritime confrontation.

All this takes place in a period of apparent détente, while conferences on European security and co-operation, and on arms reductions, are frequently in session. This leads the general public to resent any increased expenditure on defence, encouraged as they are by such Soviet statements as "The peaceful co-existence of states with differing social systems is gaining ground to an even greater extent, as are such fundamental norms of inter-state relations as respect for independence and sovereignty, equality ... and non-interference in one another's internal affairs" (Warsaw Pact Communiqué).

For home consumption, however, Leonid Brezhnev told his people: "Considering peaceful co-existence as a special form of class struggle between the countries of Socialism and capitalism, the party stresses that it cannot lead to the peaceful co-existence of the Communist and bourgeois ideologies. On the contrary one must be prepared for the struggle between them intensifying and becoming an ever more acute form of confrontation of the two social systems." Or, in a broadcast to Africa: "What should be pointed out is that when the Soviet Union calls for disarmament, it does not have in mind countries that have become victims of aggression nor people who are waging an armed stuggle for their liberation. Disarmament by the Soviet Union would jeopardise not only the existence of the Soviet Union but would reduce its support to the national liberation struggles of the Afro-Asians and Latin American peoples."

Soviet foreign policy has not altered in these fundamental principles since Lenin.

Conclusions

The Arab oil producers' action in restricting supplies and increasing prices has caused an unprecedented situation which affects not only all industrialised nations but those of the Third World. This comes at a time when all developed nations face growing inflation, which generates public pressure to cut defence expenditure. Modern communications and the mass media emphasise the growing division between rich and poor and thus encourage the cult of violence, which ranges from hijacking aircraft to guerilla warfare or military revolution.

This is the background from which our four experts have examined the problems of the Indian Ocean area, now the heart-land of the world.

Looking at the interest of the US in this vast area which has so far been of little concern to America, Mr Harrigan concludes that, while the primary US interest has to do with oil, the country's growing energy and minerals crisis demands for its solution unimpeded access to strategic minerals and materials in Africa, as well as to Middle East oil. There is also the rivalry between the two super-powers, the US withdrawal from South East Asia and the Soviet move into the Indian Ocean being the latest manifestations of this competition. Many of the most populated nations of the world, whose territories surround or are adjacent to the Indian Ocean, are watching to see who will win this strategic and psychological struggle, and will adjust their policies accordingly.

Mr. Wall has laid stress on the vital importance of Middle East oil supplies to the nations of Europe, particularly those in the NATO alliance, and concluded that until alternative supplies are developed, the long and vulnerable route to Europe round the Cape could well be the weakest link of the NATO defence system. The strengthening of this link must depend on the provision of greater maritime forces and the close co-operation of the Republic of South Africa.

The Report by The Institute of the Study of Conflict has re-stated the aims of both the USSR and the Peoples Republic of China as far as this area is concerned, underlined the difficulties facing the West in protecting the oil supplies and suggested various economic formulae by which a compromise between the desires of the Arabs and those of the West can be reached. It concluded by stressing the importance of improving relations between the "black nations" and the white-dominated south and ended by stating that this can best be achieved "if the problems and achievements of the Southern African States can first be ventilated instead of being smothered, as at present, by a world campaign of misinformation".

The fourth contributor, Mr. Adie, looked at these problems from an Australian perspective. He laid greater stress on the future of the Indian sub-continent and of South East Asia and, perhaps most important of all, pointed to the emerging power of the People's Republic of China. Soviet-Chinese rivalry may prove to be the major factor in determining the future course of world history. In certain circumstances it could also assist the West in recovering from their present position of weakness and indecision.

None of these writers saw or discussed each other's contribution, yet each, in his own way, has arrived at the same fundamental conclusions, which may perhaps be summarised as:-

1. Until alternative sources are available, the U.S. and, even more so, Western Europe and Japan are dependent on Middle Eastern oil. It can be assumed that this dependence will last for at least the next decade.
2. The requirement for oil has been highlighted and made more difficult by the action of oil producing states in restricting supplies and increasing prices at a time when industrialised nations are facing growing inflation in their own economies.

3. The effect of the oil situation on the economies of the Third World could be catastrophic and can only heighten tension between the "haves" and the "have-nots"
4. The contributors have set out to deal with the politico-military rather than the economic aspects of the present crisis. All are agreed that, in this context, the Indian Ocean is of great and growing importance not only to their own countries but to the Western world as a whole.
5. The oil supply problem involves the security both of the producing nations and of the supply routes from source to consumer.
6. The Gulf is the key area and is now a power-vacuum as far as the great powers are concerned.
7. Any direct intervention by a great power in this area would entail the danger of starting a third World War. Intervention is likely, therefore, to be through a third party. Even then the risks are considerable.
8. The West (and Japan's) oil supply routes from the Middle East are long and vulnerable and are open to interception by direct attack, by action through a third party or through blackmail.
9. This vulnerability will remain even when the Suez Canal is re-opened. In fact, on balance, this re-opening will be of more benefit to the USSR than to the West.
10. The sea routes can be protected only by a greater maritime effort by the West, and the only organisation that exists to carry out this task is NATO.
11. NATO's southern boundary is now the Tropic of Cancer but SACLANT has now been authorised to plan outside this area, in the Southern Atlantic and the Indian Ocean.
12. The wartime implementation of any such plans would entail close co-operation with the Republic of South Africa. This strategic fact has nothing to do with individual nations' domestic policies.
13. South Africa is the only industrialised area capable of supporting a modern defensive war in the southern

hemisphere between South America and Australia. Nations such as the Argentine, Brazil, Australia and New Zealand have common defence interests with the West.
14. At the present stage of World history African nationalism is bound to be neutral, and perhaps biased to the East rather than the West. Therefore as African nations become independent their ports and facilities cannot be counted upon in Western planning. The situation in Angola and Mozambique from the military standpoint is therefore detrimental to the West.
15. The USSR has exploited the political value of modern maritime power in the Mediterranean and is now following a similar policy in the Indian Ocean.
16. The result of the expansion of Soviet maritime power in the Indian Ocean will be closely studied by the Third World, the nations of which will adjust their policies accordingly.
17. While the short term threat to the West's sea communications comes from the USSR, the long term might be from China.
18. Only by greater unity and strength can the Western World face up to the pressures of the next decade. This will require both firm leadership and a better educated public opinion, the lack of which has been responsible for many political/military reverses during recent years.
19. The effect on Western economies should their main supply of gold fall into hostile hands would be disastrous.

It is to be hoped that these conclusions will be seriously considered by those who are responsible for the security of our respective countries, and that they will at least serve as an impetus to public debate.

Patrick Wall

Appendix I

CONSUMPTION AND PRODUCTION, 1972

	USSR, E. Europe & China	W. Hemisphere excl. U.S.A.	U.S.A.	W. Europe excl. U.K.	U.K.	Middle East	Africa, S.E.Asia excl. Japan	Japan
Consumption	8	5	16	13	2	1	3½	5
Production	9	7	11	½	—	18	7	—

Quantities are given in million barrels daily (mbd). One ton of crude oil = 7.33 barrels.

Appendix II

POSSIBLE PRODUCTION LEVELS (mbd)

Year	S.Arabia	Iran	Iraq	Kuwait	Abu Dhabi	Qatar	Libya
1973	6.6	5.6	1.8	3.3	1.2	0.5	2.2
1976	10	8	3	3.5	2.5	0.5	2.5
1980	14	9	5	3.5	4.5	0.5	3
1985	23	10	8	3.5	5.5	0.5	2.5

Source: Energy; the changed and changing scene.
G. Chandler, *Petroleum Review*, July 1973.

Appendix III

DEMAND FOR MIDDLE EAST OIL

United States	Europe	Japan
Current annual demand 3.3 mbd	Current annual demand 12.8 mbd	Current annual demand 4.2 mbd
1980 14.00 mbd	1980 19.00 mbd	1980 9.00 mbd
1985 18.00 mbd	1985 24.00 mbd	1985 12.00 mbd

Source: *Petroleum Review*, July 1973.

Appendix IV

The Naval situation around the Horn of Africa

As a base the chief potential threat is, of course Aden, with its excellent natural harbour, readily available to Marxist-orientated naval units supporting PFLOAG. It should also be borne in mind that the island of Perim (a former British coaling station), in the Straits of Bab-el-Mandeb, at the entrance to the Red Sea, is now under the control of South Yemen (PDRY) and has a very useful naval facilities; and that further north, at Hodeida, on the coast of Yemen, the Russians constructed a naval — and especially *submarine* — base some years ago. The island of Socotra, equally under PDRY control, would also *appear* to be a serious potential threat to the oil route, but in fact it has no natural harbour and is virtually useless from a naval point of view (furthermore, there is no physical PDRY presence on the island, whose inhabitants are independent and basically xenophobic).

The country that is watching the situation in Yemen and South Yemen with close attention is Ethiopia, whose main naval base is inside the Red Sea at Massawa. Until the recent Mid-East war Ethiopia had taken for granted an Israeli victory in any war with the Arabs, and therefore the effective neutralisation of the Red Sea as a revolutionary area from the Arab point of view. It is true that Ethiopia broke off diplomatic relations with Israel (the headquarters of the OAU is in Addis Ababa), but it has always maintained close links with the Israelis, and the Haifa-Eilat-Massawa-Addis route has been an important one for trade with and supplies to and from the West.

Ethiopia has not done much to develop its navy, largely for these reasons; but there is reason to believe that it is rethinking this policy in the light of recent developments. Its coastline is strategically important; it has a well-educated and well-trained corps of naval officers, as of army and air force officers, and it is certainly keeping a close watch on the opposite coast. Moreover, the Ethiopians have been careful to maintain links with both the West and Russia.

The actual "Horn of Africa", with the coastline to the north in the Gulf of Aden and to the east on the Indian Ocean, is under the control of the Democratic Republic of Somalia: it has a minor port on the Gulf of Aden at Berbera, and a more important one at the capital, on the Indian Ocean, of Mogadishu. Since the coup of 21 October, 1969, by General Barre, the regime is nominally Marxist-Socialist (see Part 3). But so far — while expressing impeccable Marxist principles — Somalia has not shown any sign of active cooperation with either Russia or China, and has tended to be Western-orientated (it recently welcomed a French minister from the Quai d'Orsay, and always bears in mind the French presence, immediately to the north, of the Territoire Francais des Afars et des Issars, with its capital and port of Djibouti). But though poor and with a small and largely nomadic population, it is in a strong bargaining position because of its strategic situation.

This must be regarded as a highly unstable area politically — especially with the questionmark that hangs over the future of Ethiopia without the guiding hand of the conservative (and now aged) Emperor Haile Selassie, watched carefully by France and the West, China and Russia.

GLOSSARY

ANC	African National Congress (South African political group)
ANZUS	Australia-New Zealand U.S. (defence pact)
ARAMCO	Arabian American Oil Company
ASEAN	Association of South-East Asian Nations
CENTO	Central Treaty Organisation (defence pact: GB, Pakistan, Turkey. *Associate*: US)
CFP	Compagnie Francaise des Petroles
CMEA	Council for Mutual Economic Assistance (Soviet bloc EEC counterpart)
COMECON	CMEA
CONOCO	Continental Oil Company (the Dubai concession)
COREMO	Successor organisation to MANU
CPI	Communist Party of India
CVI	Cape Verde Islands
FNLA	Frente Nacional de Libertação de Angola (guerilla/political movement)
FRELIMO	Frente de Libertação de Moçambique (guerilla-/political movement
GRU	Main Intelligence Directorate (attached to Soviet general staff)
IBERLANT	Iberia-Atlantic (defence area)
ILO	International Labour Organisation
IPC	Iraq Petroleum Company
IRA	Irish Republican Army
KGB	Committee of State Security (Soviet secret police)
MANU	Mozambique African National Union (political group)
MPLA	Movimento Popular de Libertação de Angola (guerilla/political movement)

NATO	North Atlantic Treaty Organisation (defence pact)
OAU	Organisation of African Unity (international forum)
OAPEC	Organisation of Arab Petroleum Exporting Countries
OPEC	Oil Producing and Exporting Countries (joint bargaining body)
PAC	Pan African Congress (South African political group)
PAIGC	Partido Africano da Independencia de Guinee e Cabo Verde (Bissau political movement)
PDRY	Peoples Democratic Republic of Yemen (South Yemen)
PERNAS	Peoples Front for the Liberation of Oman and the Arab Gulf (guerilla/political group)
PLO	Palestine Liberation Organisation (terorist group)
SACLANT	South Atlantic (defence area)
SALT	Strategic Arms Limitation Talks (sequence of East-West conferences)
SACP	South African Communist Party
SASOL	Suid Afrikannse Soetog Olie Ltd (oil and gas distribution company)
SEATO	South-East Asian Treaty Organisation (defence group)
SUMED	Suez-Mediterranean oil pipeline
SWAPO	South West African People's Organisation (political group)
SWANU	South West African National Union (political group)
TAPLINE	Trans-Arabian Pipeline (from Gulf to Lebanon)
UAE	United Arab Emirates
UNITA	National Union for the Total Independence of Angola (guerilla/political movement)
UNCTAD	United Nations Conference on Trade and Development (sequence of conference on economics of poor nations)

GLOSSARY

VLCC	Very large crude carrier (supertanker)
ZANU	Zimbabwe African National Union (Rhodesian guerilla/political group)
ZAPU	Zimbabwe African People's Union (Rhodesian guerilla/political group)

INDEX

Abadan, 118
Abdullah, Prince, 105
Abu Dhabi, 26,72,74,89,91,93,94-7; rich oil reserves, 95; defence force, 95; strained relations with Saudi Arabia, 96
Abu Dhabi Petroleum Company, 95
Abu Musa island, 94
Addis Abba, 126
Aden, 12,19,20,25,26,55,91,107 170, 175,184; gulf of, 185
Adie, W.A.C., (known as Ian), 9-10,139-62; problems seen from Australian angle, 178
Afars territory, 32
Africa, as source of essential minerals for Europe, 28; Communism in, 79
African National Committee, 46
African National Congress (ANC), 45, 81,126
Afro-Asian Peoples' Solidarity Organisation, 122
Agha Jari oilfield, 118
Ahwaz, 118
airfields, South African, Portuguese, Rhodesian, importance of, 54
Akins, James E., 71,73,89
Akrotiri airfield, 166
Al Ain oasis, 96
ALBA, 100
Alexandria, 130
Algeria, 45,79
Altena Farm, 47
American Export-Import Bank, 130
Amhara, 45
Amin, President Idi, 169; threatened to attack Tanzania, 169
Andaman Islands, 12,146,175
Andom, General Aman, 170

Angola, 14,47- 8,53,121,128,129,136, 162,171,180
'anti-colonialism', 122
Anya-Nya rebels, 81
apartheid, 125; defined and proclaimed, 49-50,53
Arab Development Bank, 100
Arab-Israeli Six Day War, 1967, 167
Arab-Israeli war, 1973, 28-9,39-40, 67,77,80,87,107,133
Arab nations, reduction in oil supplies to West by, 41,177; friendship of great importance to, 134
Arabian-American Oil Company (ARAMCO), 104,106,108-9,112; under pressure from Saudi Arabia, 109
Arabian Sea, 19
Argentine, 61,173,179
Ashland Oil Company, 134
ASEAN, 150
ASPAC, 150
Aswan Dam, 120
Atiqi, D., 135
Australia(ns), 11,21,153,159,173,179; danger from Soviet Union to, 161; Labour Party, 162; possible danger from Chinese, 162
Australia, New Zealand and United States (ANZUS), 52
Azerbaijan, 41

Bab, 96
Bab-el-Mandeb Straits, 130,184
Bahrein, 24,26,68,69,94,99 100, 102,109,112,117,175
Baldwin, Hanson W., Works, *Strategy for Tomorrow*, 27
Banda, Dr Hastings, 13,137,171
Bandar Abbas, 93,116; airfield, 25

191

Bandar Mahshahr, 114,118
Bandaranaike, Mrs. Sirimavo, 147
Bangladesh, 52,144
Bantu nations, 51
Barre, General Siad, 82,185
Basra, 113; petroleum company, 115
Beira airfield, 54,120,172
Beirut, 89,91,101
Belewa, Sir Abubakar, 14
Berbera, 83,170,185
Berlin Conference, 1884/5, 161
Berzrodny, Oleg, expulsion from Senegal, 84
Biafra, 81
Bid Boland, 118
Bierman, Admiral H.H., 123,; views on interdependence of states, 123-4
Black September Movement, (Palestinian), 88,118
Bombay, 146
Brazil, 61,173,179
Brazzaville, 58,79
Brezhnev, Leonid, 76,145,154,175,176
Brito, Almeida, 82
Bu Hasa oilfield, 96
Bubiyan island, 114
Burgan oilfield, 101
Burke, Arleigh, 34-5
Burma, 161
Burrell, Dr. R.M., 101-2; statement regarding Kuwait citizenship issue, 101-2.
Burandi, 4545; Chinese diplomatic missions expelled from, 85; genocide committed in, 169
Bushire airfield, 25

Cabinda, 47,121,129
Cabo Delgado district, 48
Cabora Bassa, 129; dam project, 48,171
Caetano, Marcello, 171
Cape Route, 9,32,51,61,67-8,87,129,130-7,165,172,174; a vital highway, 51,67-9; factors affecting security of, 69-70; speculative opinion regarding future of, 71
Cape Town, 32,69,127
Cape Verde Islands, 14,54,69,119,128, 129,172
Cape of Good Hope, 20,23,25,33,40,62, 68,119; NATO ships passing, 62
Caprivi strip, 47; massacre, 123
Case, William F., 23
Central African Republic, civil war in, 45; Chinese missions expelled from, 85

Central Treaty Organisation (CENTO), 52,173
Chagos Archipelago, 175
Chah Bahar, 116
Chandler, Geoffrey, 70-1
Chi Peng-fei, 162
Chiang Kai-shek, 153
Chinese People's Republic (CPR), 13,45,58,71,76; influence in Africa, 45; interest in Middle East and Africa, 86; policy in Africa, 120; ultimate objective, 121-2; common interests with Soviet Union, 139; movement away from para-military approach, 141; militancy in Africa and Middle East, 141; reason for 'joining the world', 149-50; need for Gulf oil, 154; penetration into Indian Ocean area, 156; supply of naval craft to Tanzania, and Sri Lanka, 157; denouncing of Japan's investment in Africa, 157; claim to Taiwan, 160; growing attention to Indian Ocean, 176
Chittagong, 175
Chou En-lai, 85,140,152,155,160
Cochin, 146
Cold War, 140,160
Communist Party of India (CPI), 145
(Communist) Socialist Workers' and Farmers' Party, 83
Conakry airfield, 12,58,82
Conclusions of contributors, 178-80
Continental Oil Company (CONOCO), 98
COREMO, 48
Cottrell, Dr. Alvin J., 24; observations regarding deployment of ships and aircraft in Indian Ocean, 24
Council for Mutual Economic Assistance (CMEA or Comecon), 145,154,
Crete, 167
Crozier, Brian, 9
Cuba, 80
Cyprus, 165-7

Dahomey, Chinese missions expelled from, 85
Daily Express, 104
Dar-es-Salaam, 26,48,120,126,151; harbour, 120
De Gaulle, Charles, 149
Détente in international relations, 159-60
Dhahran, 112
Dhofar, 26,86; subversive mini-war in, 26

INDEX

Diego Garcia, 12,20,23-4,55,146,156; importance of, 175
Diego Suarez, 12,25
Djibouti, 169,185; airfield, 25
Dominican Republic, 29
Dubai, 69,74,94-5,97-9
Dubai Petroleum Company, 98
Durban, 19,69,127
Dutch East Indian Company, 49

Economic Intelligence Unit, 115
Egypt, 13,44,79,80, indecision of, 170
Eritrean Liberation Front, 28
Ethiopia, 44-5,122,185-6; rivalry with Somalia, 45; Ogaden and Haud District, 169; diplomatic relations broken off with Israel, 185; links maintained with West and Russia, 185
Europe, dependence on Middle East states for oil, 40
European Economic Community, 10

Faisal, Ibn Abdul Aziz, King of Saudi Arabia, 72,96,100,106,133
Fao, 114
Fateh oilfield, 118
First National Bank, 130
Flight, 115
Fomenko, Valentin, arrest and deportation from Ghana, 84
Ford, President Gerald, 176
France, 12,21,32; interests in Western Indian Ocean, 32; sending aircraft to Libya and Kuwait, 169
Frento de Libertação de Moçambique (FRELIMO), 13,28,47,48,81,85, 120,128,171-2
Friendship Treaty, 1971, 144
Frolizi, 46
Fujaira, 94
Fulbright, Senator William, 104

Gach Saran oilfield, 118
Gan airfield, 12,55
Gandhi, Mrs. Indira, 145-6
Ghana, 79,81,123; expulsion of Russians from, 84
Global danger point, shift of, 34
Godakov, Vladimir, expelled from Kenya, 85
Gomez, General Costa, 172
Goncalves, Colonel, 172
Great Britain, 32; Royal Navy, 9; RAF airfields, 12; influence in Indian Ocean area, 156; equipping Iranian Navy, 169; rebellion crushed in Iraq and Iran by, 170; constitution of fleet in Indian Ocean, 175
Greece, enmity with Turkey, 166-7; importance of to West, 167
Greek Nation Guard, 166
Grivas, General George, 166
GRU, 83
Guinea, Republic of, 13,79,80,81,82; practises scientific socialism, 82
Guinea Bissau, 119,122,128,129
Gulf of Aden, 25
Gulf of Oman, 19,25
Gulf Oil Company, 129

Habshan, 96
Haile Selassie, Emperor, 170,186
Harrigan, Anthony, 9-11,19-35,177
Hodeida, 170,184
Horn of Africa, 169-71,184-6
Housego, David, 97
Hutu, 45

IBERLANT, 54
India, 12,26,52,145-6; denies facilities given to Soviet Navy, 27; offers bases for possible Soviet operation, 146; Navy supplied with Soviet submarines, 146; supports proposal for neutralization of Indian Ocean, 147
Indian Ocean, 143-8; importance of in global power game, 142; hopes to declare peace zone, 186
Indo-China, 160
Indonesia, 21,151; neutralizations unacceptable, 153; attempts made to develop independent life-style, 158
Indonesian Communist Party, 149
Institute for the Study of Conflict, 9,67-137,169; report by, 12-14,67,177
'International United Front', 141
investment possible by Gulf States, 135
Iran, 12,68,71,74,89; major conflict with Iraq, 27; will achieve considerable degree of industrialization, 27; purchase and importing of military equipment, 115-16,169; intentions not bellicose, 116-17; production and distribution of petroleum products, 117-18; special protection given to oil installations, 118
Iran, Shah of, 100,117; visit to Moscow, 155

193

THE INDIAN OCEAN AND THE THREAT TO THE WEST

Iraq, 12-13,26,44,74,102,107-8,113-15,144; a client Soviet State, 20; major conflict with Iran, 27; claim to Kuwait, 101; nationalization of some oil companies in, 115
Iraq Oil Company, 114
Iraq Petroleum Company, 154
Isa, Sheikh, 100
Iskenderun, 118
Islam, 78
Israel, 31,45
Issas' territory, 32
Italy, 21

Jackson, Senator, 104
Jakarta, 153,161
Janvier, Jacques, 79
Japan, 21,30,39-40,139,154-5; complete dependence on Persian Gulf Oil by, 21
Jerusalem, 133
Jebel Dhanna terminal, 96

Kampala, 169; strained relations with Khartoum, 169
Kaunda, President Kenneth, 120-1,136
Kenya, 169-70; possible power struggle in, 170
Kenyatta, President Jomo, 170
KGB (Committee of State Security), 83-4
Khadaffi, Colonel, 88,94,132
Khalid bin Mohammed, Sheikh, 95
Khalid, Crown Prince, 106
Kharg Island, 114,118
Khartoum, 169; strained relations with Kampala, 169
Khor-el-Amaya, 113
Khruschchev, Nikita, 78,139,161
Khuzistan Liberation Front, 114
Kidder Peabody Investment Company, 130
Kinshasa, 81,121
Kirkuk oilfield, 114
Kish airfield, 25
Kismayu, 83,170
Kissinger, Dr. Henry, 133
Konfrontasi, 149
Korea, 160
Korramshahr, 113
Kuala Lumpur, 151-2,161
Kuritsin, Yuri V., expelled from Kenya, 84
Kuwait, 26,72,74,100-3,114; basis of society, 102; dependent on Saudi Arabia for security, 103

Kuwait Oil Company, 101

Law of the Seas Conference, 173
Lee Kuan-yew, 151
Lenin, Vladimir Ilyich, 14,176
Lenin Institute, 81
Leopoldville, 81
'Liberation movements', 45
Liberia, 44
Lin Piao, Marshal, 139,141,152,157; attempts to assassinate Chairman Mao, 160
Lisbon, 54,69,171-2; coup, 124,172
Lisnave, Port of Lisbon, 69,129
Liu Shao-ch'i, 141
Lobito, 120-1,172
Lourenço Marques, 48,54,69,128,172
Luanda, 47,54,172
Lubumbashi, (formerly Elisabethville), 121
Lusaka, 46; conference, 147
Lyssykh, Ivan, expelled from Mali, 84

Madagascar, 20,25,35,119,158; Channel, 52
Makarios, Archbishop, 166
Malagasy Republic, 25
Malan, Dr. D.F., 25
Malawi, 13,120,121,136,171
Malayan Communist Party, 151
Malaysia, concept of neutralisation, 148-9; reliance on Five-Power Defence arrangement, 151
Mali, 79,80; expulsion of Russians from, 84
Malik, Adam, 150
Mao, Madame, 160
Marum oilfield, 118
Marxist-Leninist theory and teaching, 78-9,90; fundamental incompatability with Islam, 78
Masira airfield, 12,54
Massawa, 185
Matrah, 92
Mauritius, 12,20,55,175
McCain, John S.Jr., 35
Mediterranean, 165-8
Middleton, Drew, 22
Mina al Fahal, 92
Mindelo, 129
Mirbat, 90
Mobutu, President, 121,136
Mogadishu, 83,170,185
Mondlane, Dr., 48
Montreux Convention, 1922, 167

194

INDEX

Morgan Grenfell, (bankers), 97
Mormugao (Goa), 146
Moscow, 69,80,139,141
Movemento Popular de Libertaçao de Angola (MPLA), 47,81,85
Mozambique, 13,14,25,28,45, 48,53,68,119-22,125,128-9,136. 162,171,180; success achieved by Portuguese in Northern, 171; Tete District, 48,171
Mozambique African National Union (MANU), 48
Muller, Dr. H., 51; views on multi-racial society, 51
Murmansk, 167-8
Muscat, 92
Muzorewa, Bishop, 46

Nacala, 68,120,128,172
Nagololo, 48
Nasser, President Gamal Abdel, 79
National Front for the Liberation of Angola, (FNLA), 121
National Iranian Oil Company, 134
National Union for the Total Independence of Angola, (UNITA), 47,121
National Youth for the Liberation of Palestine, 88
NATREF, 125
Neto, Dr., 129
New Delhi, 153
New Zealand, 61,159,173,179
New York Times, 22
Nicobar Islands, 12
Niger, Chinese diplomatic mission expelled from, 85
Nigeria, 14; civil war in, 45; area of Sino-Soviet rivalry, 83
Nimeiry, President, 80
NIOC, 118
Nixon, Richard, 77,140,150,159
Nkrumah, President Kwame, 79,81
North Atlantic Assembly, 54
North Atlantic Treaty Organisation, (NATO), 10,19,23,28,32,34,40,52, 54,119,166-7,174; facing minerals crisis, 28; Western flank in chaotic state, 165; position weakened in Eastern Mediterranean, 167; Navies' difficulty in fulfilling primary responsibility, 174
North Korea, 155
Northwest Cape, 23
Nova Lisboa, 121

Novosti, 85
Nyassa district, 48
Nyerere, President Julius, 120,128,161

Observer, The, 116
Odessa, 81
oil, overriding importance of 19,20; enormous Western appetite for, 39-49; West's dependence on Middle Eastern, 61; statistics of oil reserves, 70-1; position of supply and demand, 73; suggestion that oil prices be linked with gold price, 75; income of Gulf States from, 134-5
oil-producing States, 74
Oman, 26,68,69,74,90-2; assistance from Soviet and Chinese, 90
Omar, Sheikh, 91-2
Operation Jaguar, 90
Organisation for African Unity (OAU), 81,121,122,126,136; Ninth Summit Conference of, 122; Liberation Committee, 132; ineffectiveness of, 173
Organisation of Arab Petroleum Exporting Countries (OPEC), 99 100,116,154
Ovambo tribe, 47

PAIGC, 81-2,129
Pakistan, 144-6
Palaver, 84
Palestine Liberation Fund, 87
Palestine Liberation Organisation (PLO), 12,87-8,115
Pan-African Congress (PAC), 45-6,126
Panikkar, K.M., 147
Paphos, 166
Patriot, 145
Peking, 69,80,86,139,142,149
Perim Island, 184
PERNAS, 151
Persian Gulf, 29-30,32,169; as focus of strategy, 19; conflicts in, 26; Middle East oil shipped to Europe from, 67
Perth, 25
Petroleum Council, 21
Petroleum Development, 92
Philippines, 149,152
Piraeus, 167
Poqo (PAC), 46
Popular Front for the Liberation of Oman and the Arabian Gulf (PFLOAG), 12,28,86,90-2,93,95,113,132,184; activities by, 92,100

195

Port Blair, 146
Port Louis, 175
Port Rashid, 98
Porto Dobela, 128
Portugal, 25,32,54; coups in, 172
Potchankin, Vitali, expelled from Mali, 84
Potekhin, Professor L.I., 78-9; declares Africa has 'vocation for socialism', 78-9
Potemkin, Guennad Petrovich, expelled from Ghana, 84
Pravda, 14,76

Qabus, Sultan, 90,92
Qaisumah, 112
Qatar, 68,74,94,100

Rabat, Ninth Summit Conference of OAU at, 122
Ras Tanura terminal, 109,112
Ras al Khaimah, 94
Rashid, Sheikh, 98
Razak, Tun Abdul, 151-2; visit to Moscow, 155
Razaleigh, Tunku, trade mission to Peking, 152
Red Sea, 32,52,68,170-1
Reunion Island airfield, 25,32
Rhodesia, 10,13,28,45-6,136,162,173; boycott of, 40
Richard's Bay complex, 127
Rivonia, 46
Riyadh, 104,107-8,135
Roberto, Holden, 121
Rumaila oilfield, 114
Rwanda, 45; genocide committed in, 169

Sabah issue, 152
Sadat, President Anwar, 80
SACLANT, 179
Sakharov, Dr., 159-60
Saldanha, 127
Salalah, 90
SALT, 150,159
São Vicente, 129
Saqr bin Sultan, Sheikh, 95
SASOL, 125
Sasolburg, 125
Saudi Arabia, 23,32,44,72-4,87,91,100, 103-13,133; importance of, 12; holds key to future oil supplies, 72-5; requirement for skilled help from abroad, 103; training of defence forces, 104; National Guard in, 106; threats from PDRY, 106-7; threats from Iran, 108; threats from Iraq, 108; security situation in, 113; development of Red Sea brines, 135

Sayegh, Yusif, 87-8
sea power, importance of, 9
Sea Routes Agreement, 53
Senegal, 84; expulsion of Russians from, 84
Senghor, President Leopold, 79
Seychelles, 12,55,175
Shafie, Tan Sri Ghazali, 151; proposes neutralization, 151
Sharjah, 94-5; Sheikh of, 94
Sharpeville, 45
Shatt-el-Arab, 113-14
Shevchenko, Georgi, expelled from Sengal, 84
Simonstown, 12,23,26; importance of to America, 23-4; Agreement, 1955, 32-3,53
Singapore, 12,20,32,51,148-9,151, 173,175; views Indian Ocean as peace zone, 148; neutralization unacceptable, 153
Sino-Soviet rivalry, 85-6,128-9,178; over Indonesia archipelago, 161
Socotra, 12,20,184
Solod, Daniel, expelled from Conakry, 81
Somali Republic, 12,13,20,26,52,55,82; rivalry with Ethiopia, 45; opted for 'scientific socialism', 82; army trained by Russians, 82; hopes to invade Ethiopia and Kenya, 169; controls Horn of Africa, 185; Western oriented, 185
South Africa, Republic of, 10,13,124-8,136,159,162,173,179; Navy, 25-6; boycott of, 40; Act, 49; policy of apartheid, 49; racial problem, 50; world's largest supplier of diamonds, 59; one of world's leading trading nations, 59-60; as country with strongest economy in Southern Hemisphere, 61; industrialization of, 124-5; possible improved relations with Angola and Mozambique, 137
South African Coal, Gas and Oil Corporation (SASOL), 125
South African Communist Party, 126
South African Financial Gazette, 23

INDEX

South East Asia Treaty Organisation (SEATO), 52,173
South West African National Union (SWANU), 47
South West African People's Union (SWAPU), 47,81
Southern Africa, 69; vital importance to the West, 13; strategic importance of, 45; problem of stability in, 136
Southern Oil Exploration Corporation (SOEKOR), 124
Soviet Union, 10-11,13,32,45,58; dispatches strong naval forces into Indian Ocean, 20,69,119,147,156,174-5; checking of ambitions by Americans, 24; possible deployment in event of crisis, 26; increase in naval forces in Indian Ocean, 35; possible intervention in dynastic dispute between Gulf States, 41; need for oil from Middle East, 41,44; expected to import high grade oils, 44; spread of influence in South East Asia, 52; increase in maritime power, 9, 52,54-5,174; first appearance of fleet in Mediterranean, 55,167; could use blackmail technique regarding NATO oil supplies, 58; second largest and most modern fleet, 62,64; as global power, 76; playing super-Power game in Middle East, 77; Middle East aims, 77-8; setting up client States, 80; aid to PAIGC, 82; representation in Middle East and Africa, 83; attitude to Iraq, 115; attitude to African states, 119; movement away from bloc concept, 140; pipeline diplomacy to be borne in mind, 142-3; idea of collective security, 145,154; possible plans to supply Europe with oil, 154; inevitably seeking help from Japan and America in developing Siberian oilfields, 154; seeking to link energy crisis with collective security, 155; treaty with India, Iraq and Egypt, 161; composition of fleet in Mediterranean, 168; efforts concentrated in Somalia, South Yemen and Yemen Arab Republic, 170
Spear of the Nation (ANC), 46
Spiers, Ronald, 35
Spinola, General Antonio de, 171-2
Sri Lanka (Ceylon), 11-12,20,55,147,157,158; proposes

Indian Ocean peace zone, 147
Stalin, Joseph, 78,140
Straits of Hormuz, 27,41,68,92-4
Straits of Malacca, 148
Strijdom, J.G., 50
Subic Bay, 175
subversion, 88-9
Sudan, 80; civil war in, 45; area of Sino-Soviet rivalry, 83; Southern disrupted by warfare, 169
Suez, 20,130,133
Suez Canal, 13,51,61,68,78,131,157,167-8,170,175,179
Suharto of Indonesia, President, 145,150; views on neutralization, 150
Sujatmoko, 149
Sulman al-Khalifa, Sheikh Isa bin, 100
SUMED pipeline, 68,130-1
Supreme Allied Commander Atlantic (SACLANT), 54
Switzerland, 152
Syria, 13,44,144

Taiwan, 29,141,153,155,173
Tan-Zam Railway, 28,58,85,120
Tanzania, 26,28,35,45,48,79,120,157; under Chinese influence, 120
TAPLINE, 109,112
Tashkent, 81
Teheran, 116
Tete, 48,171
Thailand, 149,161
Times of India, The, 145
Times, The, 88,123,134
Tomas, President Americo D. Rodrigues, 171
Treaty of Vereeniging, 49
Trincomalee, 147
Tripoli, 114
Tumbs, 94
Turkey, invasion of Cyprus by, 166; importance of to West, 167
Tutsi, 45
Tyumen oilfields, 154

Umm Shaif oilfield, 96
Umm al Qwain, 94
Umm Qasr, 12,101,114,115,175
União das Populações de Angola (UPA), 47
Union Defence Force, 95
United Arab Emirates (UAE), 27-8,74,94-5

197

United Nations General Assembly, 55,122; Afro-Asian line in, 122; International Labour Organisation, 123;
United States of America, 10-11; Navy, 9,12; development of communications station by, 20; deployment of Navy, 26; concern regarding uncertainty of oil developments, 21; increasing importing of oil from Persian Gulf visualised, 21; should develop its own domestic energy sources, 22; disadvantages in attempts to maintain access to Persian Gulf oil, 23; possible defence coordination with South Africa, 25; concern with respect to Western Indian Ocean related to need for adequate oil supplies, 28; threatened loss of energy sources, 29; lack of effective forces in Indian Ocean, 29; passivity of, 29-30; additional strength needed in Western Indian Ocean, 30; Iran, importance of relationship with, 31; needs to develop improved relations with Saudi Arabia, 31; arms sold to Saudi Arabia, Kuwait and Israel, 31,169; suggested attitude to Arab nations and Israel, 31-2; must calculate role of NATO countries, 32; wait-and-see policy of, 35; small demand for oil from Middle East sources, 73; common interests with Soviet Union, 139; Committee on Defence Production, 142; interest in Indian Ocean area, 157,177

Verwoerd, Dr. H.G., 50; pursues policy of separate development, 50
Vietnam, 51; war, 35; withdrawal of US from, 173
Vinogradov, Valter, expelled from Ghana, 84
Visakhapatnam, 146
Vladivostok, 148,167-8,175
VLCCs (Very Large Crude Carriers), 69,93-4,96,99,119,127-8,131
Vorster, B.J., 50; pursues policy of separate development, 50

Wall Major Patrick MC,MP, 9,32-3,39-64,177; states need for NATO recognition of Simonstown Agreement, 33; stresses vital importance of

Middle East oil supplies to Europe, 177
Wankie Game Reserve, 46
Whitlam, Gough, 153
Wilson, Harold, 174
'Wiriamu massacre', 123
World, The, 126

Xhosa territory, 51

Yamani, Sheikh Ahmad Zaki, 104-5,109
Yatsin, Lev, expelled from Mali, 84
Yemen, 185
Yemen, South, (PDRY), 13,52,55,90-1,106-7,113,131-2,184-5; state of friction and chaos in, 170
Young, Gavin, 116;17; comments on Iran's military build-up, 116
Yukalov, Yuri, expelled from Kenya, 85

Zahrani, 112
Zaid, Sheikh, 96-7
Zaire, 47,80,121-2,136
Zambia, 46-7,120-1,136
Zanzibar, 20,58,120
Zarrara, 96
Zimbabwe African National Union (ZANU), 46-7,85
Zimbabwe African People's Union (ZAPU), 46,81
Zululand, 125